Creating a Just Future

Jürgen Moltmann

Creating a Just Future

*The Politics of Peace and the Ethics of Creation
in a Threatened World*

SCM PRESS
London

TRINITY PRESS INTERNATIONAL
Philadelphia

Translated by John Bowden from the German
*Gerechtigkeit schafft Zukunft. Friedenspolitik und Schöpfungsethik
in einer bedrohten Welt,*
published 1989 by Christian Kaiser Verlag, Munich.

© Jürgen Moltmann 1989

Translation © John Bowden 1989

First published 1989

SCM Press Ltd
26-30 Tottenham Road
London N1 4BZ

Trinity Press International
3725 Chestnut Street
Philadelphia, Pa. 19104

British Library Cataloguing in Publication Data

Moltmann, Jürgen
Creating a just future : the politics of peace and
the ethics of creation in a threatened world.
1. Society. Role of Christianity
I. Title (Gerechtigkeit schafft Zukunft. *English*)
261.1

ISBN 0–334–01909–5

Library of Congress Cataloging-in-Publication Data

Moltmann. Jürgen.
(Gerechtigkeit schafft Zukunft. English)
Creating a just future : the politics of peace and the ethics of
creation in a threatened world / Jürgen Moltmann.
p. cm.
Translation of: Gerechtigkeit schafft Zukunft.
ISBN 0–334–01909–5 : $7.95
1. Peace — Religious aspects — Christianity. 2. Christianity and
justice. / . Human ecology — Religious aspects — Christianity.
I. Title.
BT736.4.M6613 1989
261—dc20
89–5097
CIP

Phototypeset by Input Typesetting Ltd, London
and printed in Great Britain by
Richard Clay Ltd, Bungay, Suffolk

Contents

Preface   vii

I   Does Modern Society have a Future?

1. Contradictions in modern society   1
2. Experience of God and the Christian hope
   for the future   5
3. Creating justice in society   8
   (a) Persons in community   8
   (b) Community in generations   11
   (c) Generations in the natural environment   13
   (d) Creation in the presence of God   14

II   The Nuclear Situation: The Theology and Politics of Peace

1. The shift from clear hope to apathetic anxiety   16
2. The dates of the nuclear age   19
3. New theological thought: political theology   24
4. Atomic end-time and apocalyptic hope   29
5. The nuclear catastrophe: where is God?   32
6. Hope against danger   37
7. Justice, not security, creates peace   38
8. The way to lasting peace   40

9. Taking responsibility for the enemy   42
10. Overcoming violence with non-violence   44
11. The categorical imperative of life in the nuclear age   46
12. Are Christians capable of peace?   47

III   The Ecological Situation: The Theology and Ethics of Creation

1. The ecological crisis of modern civilization   51
2. The change from one-sided domination to reciprocal
   community   55
3. The sabbath of the earth: the divine ecology   61
4. The community of creation as a community under law 66
   (a) Reconciliation with creation   66
   (b) Creatures in community under law   69
5. The psychosomatic crisis of modern men and women   71
6. The sabbath of humankind: the divine therapy   80
7. China between Tao and Mao   87
   (a) Harmony in the scheme of 'nature'   88
   (b) Progress in the scheme of 'history'   92
   (c) In search of a viable balance between equilibrium
       and progress   98

Notes   102

Preface

We tend to think that the future comes with time. That is how it used to be. But if humanity's threat to itself by atomic, chemical and biological means of mass destruction and by the rapidly developing destruction of nature becomes a total threat, then the future is no longer a matter of course, but must be deliberately 'created'. Its own life-span is within human power, and we must keep creating new respites for life if we want the life of coming generations and the life of the beings which live with us on this earth. The human race has become mortal. Our time has had a limit put on it. That is a new situation in human history, in which Christian faith and Christian theology must also find a place. As a result of this possibility of annihilation, the time in which the end of humankind and all higher living beings on this earth has become possible has taken on the character of an end-time in a banal sense which is not at all apocalyptic. In this situation it is more important to learn the new questions of life and death to which we still have no saving answers than to repeat the old answers to the questions of former generations.

Of course my experiences of this new situation are European experiences, and my way of expressing them is shaped by Western and German traditions. So I have deliberately restrained myself and have said little about the situation of people in 'Third World' countries, not because I think that they are unimportant but because we can hear theologians from the 'Third World' speak on these questions themselves. But I am convinced that the community of theologians, Christians and human beings in this one but divided world is strongest when each begins from his or her own situation. The more we commit ourselves to peace and disarmament in divided Europe, the more we will have the same intentions as those who are fighting for liberation and economic justice in the 'Third World' and help them. Solidarity also means solving our own problems in community with others and with respect to theirs.

The three chapters about social justice, the politics of peace and the ethics of creation which make up this book have arisen out of lectures which I have given and discussed in various places. Chapter I originated in the Gore Lecture which I gave in Westminster Abbey in November 1987. Chapters II and III arose out of the Hope Lectures given in Stirling, Scotland, in 1987; the ANZATS Lectures in Melbourne, Australia; the Second International Peace Seminar in Budapest in 1987; the Birks Lectures at McGill University, Montreal, in 1988; and the Homer J. Armstrong Lectures at Kalamazoo College, Michigan, in 1988. I am also giving them as the 1989 Anthony Jordan Lecture Series at Newman College, Edmonton, Canada. I hope that their publication will also help to further the progress of the conciliar formation of opinion on 'Justice, Peace and the Preservation of Creation' which was stimulated and begun at the World Council of Churches General Assembly in Vancouver in 1983.

Tübingen, 6 December 1988   Jürgen Moltmann

I

Does Modern Society have a Future?

1. Contradictions in modern society

By 'modern society' I understand in general the human societies which have arisen out of the industrial revolutions. In particular I have in mind the society of West Germany in which I live and in which my children will also live. All industrial societies are subject to permanent social change. Today we are experiencing the 'third industrial revolution': after mechanization came electrification, and now we have the computerization of production. This change in methods of production calls for mobility and flexibility on the part of men and women; they have to be capable of realizing new possibilities and strong enough to overcome the contradictions that they experience. From a social and political perspective modern industrial society is necessarily a society of permanent reforms. Only if it is ready to be transformed can this society do justice to its own possibilities.

However, for any social reform we need a historical vision, i.e. the vision of a future for which it is worth living. Particularly in times in which technological transformations are leading many people into great social conflicts and economic dangers, such a vision is vital for survival: 'Where there is no vision, the people perish' (Prov.29.18). Conservative people become incapable of the future because they are incapable of change.

They want everything to remain just as it is for them now. They want to extend their present into the future in order to defend their possessions. So they are usually afraid of a future which could look different from the present which they know. They do not hope for change, but rather are afraid of it. But those who want only to extend their present into the future neglect the new possibilities which the future offers them. With these possibilities they suppress the future itself. The simple prolongation of the *status quo* no longer provides a future for which it is worth living. Only through change and reforms will we be able to be save what we think worth saving for the future. The anxiety of Conservatives, Marxists or anti-Marxists over the future tends these days to be expressed in worry about 'destabilization'. Yet without a deliberate and planned destabilization of our own system there can be neither change (*perestroika*) nor hope for a new future. To put it more simply: no crisis, no opportunity; no criticism, no future.

Does modern society have a 'future'?

Many people who suffer under the contradictions of this society and recognize them have serious doubts. Many people who suffer from these contradictions and do not recognize them despair in an apathetic way. In general it can be said that never before in the rich societies of this earth has there been so much disorientation, resignation and cynicism, self-hatred and aggression against the institutions as there is at present in Western industrial societies. Here are some of these contradictions.

1. We live not only in class societies but also in 'two-thirds societies'. These are societies in which two-thirds of the population push the other third under the poverty line and degrade them so that they are 'surplus people', although the resources are available to make it possible for all members of our society to have a free and just life. These include children and old people, the handicapped and the uneducated, and many marginal groups. In West Germany we live with an unemployment rate of between eight and ten per cent, and

according to official government statements we have resigned ourselves to 'having to live with this structural unemployment' in the future as well, although according to Article 23 of the Universal Declaration of Human Rights 'every person has the right to work'. Ten per cent of our people are deprived not only of the possibility of earning an income adequate to support them but also of the self-respect and the community with others which is gained by work and having an income. That several of our Western industrial societies have been producing a 'new poverty' over the last decade is not an inevitable fate, but the result of neglect in the social and political sphere. It is a scandal that young people are growing up who are shown every day by growing unemployment that they are not needed. We know that there is a connection between unemployment, crimes against property and prison sentences. Fifty per cent of all criminal prisoners in the USA were unemployed at the time they committed their crime. Since 1979 there has been an increase of sixty per cent in burglaries in West Germany. Our society is coming to its end in these young people: 'No future' is their desperate response.

2. Those who have hope for the future save in the present and invest in the future. Those who have no hope and do not want a future enjoy the present and create debts which their children or others will have to pay at a later date. One can see clearly the hope and hopelessness of a society from its investments and debts. Our Western societies are in no way just creditor countries for the increasingly indebted countries of the Third World, but are themselves accumulating enormous deficits in national budgets, above all in the USA. In this way we are burdening our children and their children with horrendous debts and making life difficult for them. This is 'politics without a future' – 'no-future politics'.[1]

3. To protect themselves against one another, modern societies have devised and built up the 'system of nuclear deterrence'. Out of fear of mutual destruction, more and more resources are being devoted to 'security' – from the atom bomb to 'Star

Wars'. 'Mutually assured destruction' is meant to guarantee security. But the more resources are expended on this 'security', the less value there is in what is meant to be secured. The nuclear deterrent threatens not only the potential opponent but also the whole of humanity and all higher life on earth with annihilation. It contains the threat of global mass murder. Humankind as a whole has become mortal, and there are two or three political and military systems which decide whether humanity goes under or survives. We have to accept the view of the philosopher Günter Anders that with Hiroshima and Nagasaki in 1945 the possible end of humanity has begun: the end of the future is possible at any time.

4. Not least, modern industrial society has produced more riches than any society before it. But it is producing these riches for humankind at the expense of nature. No previous human society has irretrievably destroyed so much of the natural environment as this society. The 'ecological crisis' into which our societies have led nature and human beings has presumably already become an 'ecological catastrophe', at any rate for the weaker forms of life.[2] Those who are aware of this live in the tormenting fear that nature could decay to the point when humankind could one day join the dinosaurs as an extinct form of life. And what makes these thoughts so disturbing is the suspicion that the decision could already have been made irrevocably, because we can no longer retrieve the poisons which are rising into the ozone layer or sinking into the ground. In that case the fate of humankind would already be sealed before the symptoms of its extinction made themselves felt. In that case we would in fact no longer have a future but only a present, which within a foreseeable space of time would become past.

Have Christians a 'vision of hope' for this world, or is established Christianity so fused with our society that we not only share the ambiguities and contradictions of this society but also no longer have any message of hope to offer to our contemporaries? In a pluralistic society the church of Christ

4

certainly does not have the right to speak for all men and women, Christians and non-Christians. But all men and women in this society have the right to hear what Christians have to say as Christians, i.e. on the basis of their particular belief and their all-embracing hope.

Not many people expect established Christianity as it is experienced by people in our society to have a vision of hope of a future which is worth living for. That is true. But is the true church of Jesus Christ not the reality of a return to God and the reality of the experience of rebirth to a living hope and in the unity of conversion and rebirth the sacrament of God's future and the future of the world? I find that that is even more true. I do not know any reason for being a Christian other than this divine experience of conversion, rebirth to a living hope and the presence of the kingdom of God in the Spirit of God.

2. Experience of God and the Christian hope for the future

When Christians think about the future of this society which is threatened by death, they begin with the experience which makes them Christians. When the church intervenes in the conflicts of the society in which it lives, it does so for the sake of God, to whom it owes its existence. The social commitment of Christians is witness to Christ, and the political responsibility of the church arises out of the innermost nucleus of its divine commission. Otherwise both of these would remain arbitrary and in rrinciple superfluous. But what makes Christians Christians and the church the church of Christ?

1. It is the action of God through Christ which brings about justification and creates peace among us unjust and peaceless people. 'Christ was put to death for our sins and raised for our justification,' says Paul in Romans 4.25. And the same thing is said of peace in Colossians 1.19-20: '... and through him (Christ) to reconcile to himself all things, whether on earth or in heaven, making peace by the blood of his cross'. All that determines

5

being a Christian, and all that the church is and can do, is indebted to this action of God in Christ which makes just, reconciles and creates peace. So the church is nothing other than the fruit of the reconciling suffering of God and the creation of the justifying action of God, and in the unity of both these is the work of the will of God which creates peace and gives life. What in faith we experience as 'church' has time and again been described as the experience of grace, the divine acceptance and establishment of those who give themselves up because they no longer see any future for themselves.

2. However, out of each gift there arises a corresponding task. If the church, if Christians, are the work of the action of God which creates justice and makes peace, then they are also and equally seriously the instrument of this divine action in this world. From the justification of the unjust there follows their mission with a commitment to better justice in society. From the reconciliation of those who are not at peace there follows a mission to create peace in the conflicts of this society. There cannot be any other response by Christians to their experience of God. The creative action of God and the action of human beings in response to that are indeed not on the same level, since God is God and human beings are human beings. But no one may separate these two levels which God himself has brought together. As human beings wholly owe their justice to God, so God is utterly concerned with just human action. When God justifies men and women he puts the hunger and thirst for righteousness in their hearts. God gives us his peace in order to make us peacemakers. Anyone who is personally satisfied with the peace of God for his or her own person and does not become a peacemaker does not know the dynamics of the Spirit of God.

The church exists in modern society as the work and instrument of God's justice. The economic, political and social conflicts of this society are also its own conflicts. Christians experience them in their own bodies. The more strongly they believe in the justice of God, the more painfully they suffer

6

over the injustice that they see. If there were no God, then perhaps one could accept violence and injustice, because that was the way things were. But if there is a God and this God is just, then one can no longer accept them. In that case we can never become accustomed to injustice, but will have to contradict it and resist it with all the powers at our disposal. If there is a God, then there is a justice and judgment which no one escapes.

The more accurately a church recognizes its social context, the more effectively it can become an instrument of God's justice in society. Political theology in Europe and liberation theology in Latin America have sharpened our awareness of our social and political context. That has nothing to do with a dubious left-wing 'politicization of the church', as some suspect, but is solely in the service of the church's public testimony to Christ and the responsibility which every Christian takes on in the face of God's righteousness.[3]

3. If the church is the work and the instrument of God's justice in the world, then it is also the beginning and the pledge of the coming new creation of the world in this justice. If the peace of God is also experienced in the church, then hope for 'peace on earth' also arises here. Faith responds with thoughts, words and deeds to the justice of God which it experiences, and hope expects the new just world. Faith accepts peace with God, but hope anticipates the new world of peace. Faith finds the comfort of God in all suffering, but hope looks into the future of a new creation in which there will no longer be any suffering, pain or crying. To put it simply: anyone who believes in God has hope for this earth and does not despair. We look beyond the horizon of the apocalyptic terrors into the new world of God and act accordingly.

Since Uppsala 1968, in ecumenical discussions we have called this life in hope 'life in anticipation': prepare the way of the Lord. Though anxieties and fears have grown greater today, I think that the message of Uppsala is as topical as ever – and indeed even more important:

7

We call on you in the trust of God's renewing power to participate in the anticipation of God's kingdom and already today to show something of the new creation which Christ will complete on his day... God renews, and Christ wills that his church should now already be a sign and the announcement of a renewed, human society.

Human beings do not live by traditions but also in anticipations. In fear and in hope we anticipate the future and commit ourselves to it in the present. Those who despair today and say 'No future' anticipate their end and destroy the life of others. But Christians anticipate the future of the new creation, the kingdom of justice and freedom, not because they are optimists but because they trust in the faithfulness of God. Certainly we shall not realize the kingdom of righteousness in the world. But we cannot dispense ourselves from this task for God's sake. An anticipation is a foretaste, a sign of hope and a beginning of new life.

3. Creating justice in society

I now want to consider the essential relationships in human life from the perspective of God's justice and peace, which serve life.

I shall do so in the following order:

(*a*) Persons in community
(*b*) Community in generations
(*c*) Generations in the natural environment
(*d*) Creation in the presence of God

(a) Persons in community

Modern industrial society has produced that public individualism in which each person is concerned with his or her own freedom and no one cares too much about others. As a result of the principle of competition the capable are rewarded and the weak punished. When in addition opportunities, professions and jobs are in principle kept scarce, the result is a struggle of all against all, since 'there is never enough for everyone'. The result is a society of the upwardly mobile, in which more and more people are forced to the margin or oppressed. The ideology of 'there is not enough for everyone' makes people lonely, isolates them, deprives them of their relations with others and leads them to social death.

If people in our society are again to be able to live more human lives, then we must build up communities from below and recognize that we can only develop our personalities in relationships and communities. The alternative to poverty is not property. The alternative to poverty and property is community. The principle of life is called 'mutual help', as Kropotkin already demonstrated against Charles Darwin in the animal and human world. In communities we become rich: rich in friends, in neighbours and colleagues, brothers and sisters, on whom we can rely in emergencies. Together, as a community, we can help ourselves in most difficulties. Together, in solidarity, we are strong enough to shape our destiny. But if we are divided, then we can also be controlled under the old Roman rule 'Divide and conquer'. Therefore the community is the true protection of personal freedom.

However, conversely we must recognize that the community is always conservative, while individuals can be creative. Human individuals develop in community, and the human community changes in persons.

Modern society is everywhere a centralized society. It has created the great industrial and administrative centres in the conurbations. As a result it has impoverished the local communities and emptied the countryside. The rebuilding of human society will therefore begin with local communities which can be seen and experienced and will restore to the local communities many functions and tasks which have been centralized. In a time of modern means of communication, decentralization is not a technical problem. Society is human and viable in independent communities.

The same goes for the established church, at any rate in West Germany. We have taken mission, ecumenical relationships and diaconia from local communities and delegated them to large organizations. This has made the local community poor and passive. The delegation of tasks which one can do oneself leads to alienation. So we are now returning these tasks to the local community in order that the local communities can be diaconal, missionary and ecumenical communities. The local communities can themselves care for many of their handicapped and old members once they become living communities instead of religious liturgical communities. That is what was said of the first Christian community in Jerusalem (Acts 4.32ff.): 'The company of those who believed were of one heart and soul... they had everything in common... and there was not a needy person among them.' I do not see this as a utopia, but rather as a divine promise of the Spirit which we too can experience.

The problem of unemployment is also to be seen in this context. Work is a fundamental condition of human life. It secures the material capacity to live, but in addition it brings social recognition and personal self-respect. It forms the personality. So the 'right to work' is not just a material right but also a deeply personal one. The way in which we work and distribute the opportunities for work therefore governs not only our personal destiny but also our common future.

To advocate justice in the various sphere of work therefore means at least:

1. The just distribution of the possibilities of work to women and men by shortening working hours and creating new jobs;

2. Just remuneration for work and humane organization of jobs;

3. Wide opportunities for training workers and furthering their education;

4. Instead of shortening working life the institution of sabbatical years during working life; and finally

5. The social recognition of work which people perform outside the paid sector, above all housework and work with children and old people in families.

We need a new definition of work: generally speaking, work is active participation in the social process, not in the productive process of society. Any honorary work in the social process needs public recognition, including payment.

(b) Community in generations

We have evidently become accustomed to looking at human life as a cross-section: all men and women at one time. But any look at the Old Testament shows us that former cultures looked at human life over its length: all men and women in the sequence of generations. In fact people are not only social beings; they also come in generations. They are created as generations. They live with one another and for one another as generations. Therefore human life stands and falls with the preservation or breach of the contract between the generations which is unwritten but lies at the basis of all life. This contract between the generations says that parents look after children when these are small and need help, and that children care for parents when these are old and need help. And this does not just apply to families, but to all people in the generations which live together in a society. Because everyone lives in the chain of generations and owes his or her life to it, everyone is also obliged to care for the old and the young generations. Solidarity is also experienced in the community of generations who care for one another: not just in the partnership of men and women but also in the solidarity of old and young.

Nowadays there is not only a personal and collective selfishness, but also the selfishness of the present generation about the generations to come. Human community can exist in the chain of generations only if there is a just balance of opportunities between present and future generations. Today there is the threat of a breach of the contract between gener-

11

ations which can be fatal for humankind. We are in the process of consuming in this generation the bulk of the oil available on earth. In the public budgets of communities, cities and nations we are leaving behind a tremendous mountain of debt which the coming generations must pay off. We are depositing poisonous industrial waste in the earth which our children must dig out again and dispose of properly. Our nuclear power plants are producing nuclear waste which, depending on the half-life of the material, must be stored and guarded until the year 3000 or 5000 or even longer. And not least, in contrast to all the other societies that we know of, in the future there will be more old people and less young ones in our societies. The pension contributions which the young people must pay for the old will rise. In a word, the present generation is making life very difficult for the generations to come. We are not treating our children fairly.

In order to bring justice to the sequence of generations, we will have to make cost-benefit analysis in business management more honest. It is wrong for the profits to be consumed now and the costs paid for by the generations to come. According to the basic law of the Federal Republic of Germany property entails 'social obligations'. Anyone who acquires and owns possessions and property takes on social responsibilities. And since these possessions and this property are owned in the context of the succession of generations in time, they therefore entail 'hereditary obligations'. We have to pass on land, air and water to the coming generations in the state in which we received them. Every order of possession must be related to the contract between generations, because possessions and property can only be used justly if there is also concern for the generations to come. In former agricultural societies it was taken for granted that the land one had inherited would be handed on to one's children intact. In modern industrial societies this hereditary justice between the generations has to be established deliberately, because it is no longer taken for granted and because many people no longer see the connections.

The human generations form the community of humankind in time, and the community of humankind in time exists as a succession of generations. This community in time is truly human community if there is justice between the generations and if the 'contract between the generations' is observed. In our present situation we need to honour above all the right of the child and the rights of the coming generations to life, because the children are the weakest links in the chain of generations, and the generations to come still have no voice and therefore become the first victims of present injustice.[4]

(c) Generations in the natural environment

The next context which we can now recognize is the natural environment and the relationship between human culture and the nature of the earth. Men and women are not just social beings and beings in generations, but also natural beings. They belong to nature and are dependent on nature. Human civilizations can only develop in equilibrium with the cosmic conditions of the earth as an organism. If they destroy it, then human civilizations will die out. The pre-modern agricultural societies were aware of this and also respected these conditions of the earth by their animistic cosmic piety. It is modern industrial societies which have detached themselves from the laws and rhythms of nature. They were solely built up on human wishes and conceptions. Modern scientific and technological civilization is the first civilization which has simply subjected and exploited nature. Francis Bacon had prophesied that science and technology would make nature the 'slave of humankind', and René Descartes boasted that human beings would make themselves the 'maître et possesseur de la nature' through the natural sciences and technology. But nature protests against its rape by modern industrial society through its silent death or through counter-evolutions like Aids, algae and so on. In such a collapse human beings will die out. The earth will survive without them.

Only an extensive change in the life-style of human beings and in the forms of industrial production could ward off the ecological death of humankind. We need an ecological reform of our society, of production, of consumption and of transport. It is technically quite possible if there is the political will. All human property, especially large-scale industrial property and transportation systems, need to be examined for their 'environmental compatibility'. Anything that burdens or destroys the natural environment must be dismantled, or must be banned. Production of non-biodegradable consumer goods like certain chemical products and plastics cannot be continued. The waste-producing life-style in the prosperous countries must be shown up as being 'unnatural' and 'unhealthy' and reformed in favour of a natural and healthier life-style. Ecological justice, which is the basis of a symbiosis of humankind and nature capable of survival, will become just as important in the future as economic justice and justice between the generations.

The ecological reform of our society also begins in the small communities that we can keep an eye on. Only outsiders do not worry about the destruction of the environment. Those who have to live in the environment preserve it and keep it fit to live in. Therefore citizens' action groups are rightly coming into being to combat the major industrial projects of foreign, multinational concerns which destroy nature.

(d) Creation in the presence of God

To return to inner human attitudes: above all we need a new respect for nature and a new reverence for the life of other creatures. This is where I see the great task of the religions and above all of the Christian church, since it was the Western 'religion of modernity' which opened up the way for the secularization of nature. At the end of a long history of our civilization, the old world-view in terms of harmonious natural forces has been destroyed, on the one hand through modern monotheism and on the other by the mechanism of the natural sciences. Modern monotheism has deprived nature of its divine mystery and eliminated magic, as Max Weber pointed out. It has made nature the material for human conquest. If there is to be new respect for nature and a new reverence for the life of

14

religion of modernity

other creatures, then this 'religion of modernity' must be fundamentally reformed. We shall no longer be able to separate God and nature but will see God in nature and nature in God. We shall reintegrate ourselves into the all-embracing community of creation from which we had detached ourselves. We shall understand again that nature and we ourselves are God's creation, and we shall resist human destruction of nature in the name of the divine creation. So we shall no longer just want to know nature in order to dominate it, but want to understand it in order to take part in it. We shall accord non-human nature rights in the ecological reform of our society and take note of the rights of our fellow creatures. We shall rediscover the wisdom of God in nature, of which Proverbs 8 says: 'He who finds me finds life, but he who sins against me destroys his own soul. All who hate me love death.' This is where I see the greatest and most urgent task for contemporary theology. And I see the greatest task of the church of Christ today as being the ecological reformation of the 'religion of modernity'. The presupposition for an ecological shift in modern industrial society is a spiritual and cultural shift which has its roots in a new religious experience of the reality of God and of nature.

Does modern society have a future?

Its future is repentance.

Will humankind survive the crises that I have described? We cannot know and we may not know. If we knew that humankind would not survive, then we would not do anything more for our children, but say 'After us the flood.' If we did know that humankind would survive, then we would also do nothing, and we would neglect our opportunity of conversion by doing nothing. Because we cannot know whether humanity will survive, we must act today as though the future of all humankind depended on us, and at the same time trust wholly that God will remain true to his creation and not let it fall.

15

II

The Nuclear Situation: The Theology and Politics of Peace

1. The shift from clear hope to apathetic anxiety

On 28 August 1963, Martin Luther King stood in front of the Lincoln Memorial in Washington and proclaimed to a divided and oppressed world his unforgettable dream of peace, freedom and humanity:

> I have a dream that one day this nation will rise up and live out the true meaning of its creed, 'We hold these truths to be self-evident, that all men are created free and equal.' I have a dream that my four little children will one day live in a nation where they will not be judged by the colour of their skin, but by the content of their character.
>
> I have a dream that one day 'every valley shall be exalted and every hill and mountain shall be made low... and the glory of the Lord shall be revealed, and all flesh shall see it together'.[1]

In October 1983, not far from that very place, at the White House, President Ronald Reagan must also have had a dream. In reply to questions from a Jewish correspondent of the *Jerusalem Post*, he answered:

> I return to your prophets of the Old Testament and to the signs which announce Armageddon and I ask myself if we are not the generation that will experience this. I don't know

16

if you have noticed any other prophecies recently, but believe me, they definitely describe the time in which we live.

During the election campaign Mr Reagan was asked by Marvin Kalb whether by that he meant a 'nuclear Armageddon'. He first answered in the affirmative, but then confused the issue in vague, non-committal talk.[2]

Little characterizes the change in the mood of the time better than these two visions, which lie only twenty years apart and which each in its own way has influenced the world. The Civil Rights Movement in the USA came to a climax with Martin Luther King. The overcoming of centuries-old racism in temperament and law became possible and then real, thanks to the rebirth of this messianic hope of the coming glory of the Lord which unites divided and hostile humankind. And already here and now this messianic hope gave people the hope to overcome hatred and enmity. 'We shall overcome – some day. Deep in my heart I do believe, we shall overcome – some day,' we sang at that time – and not just in the USA.

This has obviously now changed radically. The horrible nightmare of the bloody final battle at Armageddon has replaced the political vision of the hope for life, freedom and justice – and not only at the White House in Washington. A new spectre has also been going around in Europe, particularly since Chernobyl, the spectre of the nuclear apocalypse. For these years 'Apocalypse Now' is not just a film title. People everywhere are hearing the bells of the world clock strike for the last time. The plans of ministries for 'the day after' sound like unimaginable horror stories. In the 'five minutes to midnight' which still remain to humankind doctors have to learn 'triage' to select those who are hopelessly contaminated by radiation. Large quantities of psycho-pharmaceutical drugs are being stored in readiness – for example in a psychological hospital in Tübingen – to tranquillize patients in panic and to put the incurably injured to sleep. The anticipation of apocalyptic infernos through such scenarios of 'catastrophe medicine' have their effects, above all in the growing pessimism of the young generation: No future![3]

What effect does that have?

Intellectually as well as in practice, people are digging themselves in, walling themselves up and keeping quiet. They are simply interested that nothing should change: no real disarmament in the military system; no reform in the economic system. They are fixated on the present and there is no longer another future. Therefore the present must be stretched and extended as far as possible. Any real alteration in conditions could unbalance the whole structure and topple it into the abyss. So any motivation towards a new start and a change of the obsolete conditions by virtue of a new future hope is evidently a thing of the past.

For whose advantage? For whose benefit are these pictures of terror? The pictures of terror in the new apocalypse exclusively serve the so-called 'politics of security'. The politics with which if need be justice and constitution are abolished in many countries, human rights are infringed and large parts of the poor are impoverished to safeguard the rich, and which in terms of Realpolitik are called 'politics of national security', have become the politics of modern apocalyptic. The hopeful start for 'new frontiers' of social justice has given place to the resigned acceptance of the imminent, unavoidable final battle with the 'kingdom of evil' in Armageddon.[4]

However, it is paradoxical that this new mood of the downfall of the world hardly makes any difference to the way in which many people live: it does not make any difference to their middle-term holiday plans. If you ask people what they expect in the next twenty years, you will get contradictory answers: in political terms many people expect an atomic war in this generation, but hardly anyone has personal expectations of his or her own death. Many people expect devastating ecological catastrophes, but hardly anyone personally expects a terminal disease. These contradictions are difficult to interpret: the apocalyptic mood of the time is politically effective and can be

18

exploited, and it also preoccupies many people when they think of the future of the world, but it remains on the surface of personal life and does not bring about any changes. It makes people sensitive, but it also dulls them. It alarms but does not stimulate. It should lead to decisions in time, but by the general sense of catastrophe which it generates it only furthers the general lack of resolution. People are prepared to accept many negative things before the collapse of the world that they fear: they put up with injustice and violence against which they would otherwise have offered outraged opposition. The apocalyptic mood of the time leads only a few to 'watch and pray', while most lapse into a dull brooding, into 'nuclear numbing', since there is little that puts people to sleep so effectively as absolute despair. 'Could you not watch with me one hour?' Christ asked his disciples in Gethsemane.

2. The dates of the nuclear age

As early as 1946 Albert Einstein wrote the prophetic words: 'The power of the atom that has been unleashed has changed everything but my way of thinking. We need an essentially new way of thinking if the human race is to survive.' Today, more than forty years later, the destructive power of nuclear weapons has increased beyond all measure, but we are still looking for a 'new way of thinking' in order to avoid this deadly danger to humankind.[5] Since Hiroshima 'the bomb' has changed the world at a stroke, but Christian theology is only slowly becoming aware of the new situation in which all its traditional concepts for dealing with power, terror and war have become antiquated. Rockets are launched faster than the speed of sound, but the Spirit is still going on foot. Therefore the human consciousness is still lagging behind the real changes in the conditions of human existence in the nuclear age. Because we have not understood this situation realistically, we cannot yet understand the future in convincing visions of hope. The dark cloud of 'nuclear numbing' presses on human consciousness. Anxiety at the great catastrophe makes us incapable of doing what is necessary today so that our children can live tomorrow.

1. Hiroshima 1945 fundamentally changed the quality of human history: our time has become time with a deadline. The era in which we exist is the last era of humankind, for we live in a time in which an end can be put to humankind at any moment. The system of nuclear deterrence which has been constructed and increasingly perfected has made it possible to end the life of the majority of human beings in a few hours. The nuclear winter which will follow a war with nuclear weapons also gives the survivors no chance. This time when the end of humankind is possible at any moment is, in a purely secular sense and without apocalyptic pictures, in fact the end time, for no one can expect that this nuclear age will be followed by another age in which this deadly threat to humankind will no longer exist.[6] Gorbachev's dream of 'a world without nuclear weapons' is a fine dream, but it is only wishful thinking. No one seriously thinks that human beings will one day again be incapable of doing what they can do now. Anyone who has learned the formula cannot forget it again. Since Hiroshima 1945, humankind has lost its 'nuclear innocence' and will never get it back again.

If the nuclear age is the last age of humankind, then the battle for human survival today is the battle for time. The battle for life is the battle against the nuclear end. We attempt to make our end-time as end-less as possible by giving threatened life on this earth continually new reprieves. This battle over putting off the end is a permanent battle for survival. It is a battle without victory, a battle without end – in the best instance. We can prolong this nuclear end-time, but we and all future generations must live out life in this end-time under the sword of Damocles: the bomb. The life-span of the human race is no longer guaranteed by nature, as before, but must be created by the human race through a deliberate policy of survival. Previously nature has regenerated the human race after epidemics and world wars. Previously nature protected the human race from annihilation by individuals. From now on that is no longer the case. Since Hiroshima, the human race as a whole has 'become mortal', as Mikhail Gorbachev rightly said. In his view, since Hiroshima 'immortality', or more modestly 'life', has undeniably become the first task of human culture, including political culture. That means that all decisions today must be made with the life of generations to come in view. This is a new responsibility for all humankind which has been unknown hitherto.

2. The nuclear age is the first common age for all peoples and all human beings. Since Hiroshima the many different histories of the peoples of this earth have become the one, common world history of the one humankind; but to begin with, this has happened only negatively, in mutual threat and the common danger of annihilation. Granted, nuclear armament grew out of the struggle for world-domination between the super-powers: the first to become a nuclear power took a leap into the absolute. It became omnipotent through the threat of world annihilation for everyone else. But because there was no nuclear monopoly, no one won. The nuclear super-powers neutralized each other and became helpless, since 'the one who shoots first is second to die'. The nuclear deterrent has created a situation in which nothing can move. The oppressors have become the oppressed. The situation of mutual deterrence limits the scope of any great-power politics. Nuclear weapons cannot even be used for military purposes in minor conflicts. The threat to use them was of no help in Korea, in Vietnam, in Afghanistan, or in Nicaragua. Humankind has come to a dead end. Is there an alternative to the nuclear Armageddon of the super-powers? Some are thinking of a new defence system in space (the Strategic Defence Initiative, 'Star Wars'). But as there is a new attack system for every new defence system, this development does not get us out of the cul-de-sac.

The nations have now entered into the first common age of humankind, because they have all become the possible common object of nuclear annihilation. In this situation the survival of humankind is conceivable only if the nations organize themselves into a collective object of action for survival. Since Hiroshima, human survival has been indissolubly bound up with the uniting of the nations in a common defence against these deadly dangers. Only the unity of humankind guarantees survival, and the survival of each individual presupposes the uniting of humankind. If humankind is to be united in the age of nuclear threat in order to save life, what is needed is a relativization of the individual interests of nations, the democratization of ideologies which lead to conflict, tolerance of the different religions and a general subordination of all to the common interest in life.

The ongoing competition of the super-powers and the differing social systems still get in the way of the world organization we need. Nevertheless a gradual international network of political responsibility for peace in regional security partnerships is possible, as for example between the two German states and the states of Western and Eastern Europe. There are concrete steps from confrontation to co-operation.

3. The military system of nuclear deterrence is ambivalent in itself. It does not just secure peace but to a considerable degree endangers it. It can only be a transition to another way of securing peace, namely a political way. But it also endangers peace in other respects:

(a) The high level of armaments in the northern hemisphere is a burden on the peoples of the Third World, who are being increasingly impoverished and getting into debt. It has led to the arming of the developing countries and to the extension of numerous wars to these countries, as is shown by the 1986 United Nations Report on Disarmament and Development. Seventy-five per cent of the arms trade in the last two decades has been with the developing countries. Both crises are interrelated in many ways: without disarmament there can be no justice in the South, and conversely, only by the establishment of lasting developments in the South will we achieve disarmament and peace. A war with nuclear weapons is a possible danger for humankind. But the economic North-South conflict is a reality in which people are dying even now.

(b) A nuclear war would be the worst environmental catastrophe which human beings could bring about. But the high degree of armaments in the First World is also extending ecological catastrophes into the Third World – together with other factors – as a result of the impoverishment of the Third World. For exploitation creates poverty, poverty leads to debt, debt compels the sale and the consumption of natural foundations of life: the deforestation of the rain forests, the overgrazing of pastures, the expulsion of rural populations, and so on. Arms races produce poverty and destruction of the environment all over the world. Humankind is losing the capital it needs: the raw material and work forces that it requires as well as scientific intelligence for its own survival. 'Armament is theft', said President Eisenhower at the end of his time of office – rightly, as the 1987 Brundtland Report on 'Our Common Future' showed.[7] The 'spiral of mutual anxiety' led through mutual deterrence to the militarization of public awareness and the modern 'arms culture'. Not least, however, this is fatal for the human race and nature. So we must demolish this weapons-anxiety culture and create reasonable trust through democratization.

(c) Not least, attention must be drawn to the human problem of the technology of nuclear power: accelerated construction of nuclear power technology, both military and peaceful, evidently overlooks both the ecological problem of the removal of atomic waste and the 'scrapping' of nuclear bombs and the human factor in using this technology. Obviously radioactive material cannot simply be returned to nature and be dismantled by it; it must be stored somewhere and watched over for thousands of years. Moreover nuclear power technology calls for infallible human beings because it reacts in such an unfriendly way to human mistakes. Can this dangerous technology be controlled by fallible and corruptible people? The

catastrophes of Windscale/Sellafield, Harrisburg and Chernobyl and the various international corruption scandals of the
German nuclear industry say no. The experimental method,
the 'trial and error method', comes up against particular limits.
We can no longer make any major errors, either meltdowns in
nuclear power stations or a nuclear war. But that means that
we cannot try any more experiments. We only live once. It only
needs one major nuclear accident or nuclear war and there will
be no one left to become wise as a result of the experience. And
that means that either human beings must withdraw from the
deadly technology of nuclear power and look for other sources
of energy which are more compatible with the environment
and friendly to human beings, or they must be abolished or
reconstructed genetically to be different from those of whom
it used to be said so graciously, 'to err is human'. The end
of experimental genetic technology is also in sight: bacteria
produced by genetic engineering cannot be recaptured once
they are exposed. Such action is unique and irrevocable.
One cannot learn from the damage. We are opening up
developments which get out of control. We are making free
decisions through which we are losing our own freedom. Once
the decisions are final, irrevocable and unrepeatable, then we
no longer have experiments. And then there is no more room
for possibility. In that case truth and error can no longer be
distinguished. We get to the position where it is all or nothing.
But in this way we come to the end of time and into the eternal
presence of what was traditionally called the 'Last Judgment'.

3. New theological thought: political theology

The new political theology came into being in Germany after
the end of the war under the devastating shock of Auschwitz.[8]
For us young Germans who began theology after the war,
'Auschwitz' became the turning point for our thought and
action. We became painfully aware that we had to live inescap-

24

ably 'after Auschwitz' and in the shadow of the holocaust which had been inflicted in the name of our people on the Jewish people. 'After Auschwitz' became the concrete context for our theology as well. With the name of the place of the atrocity we denoted not only a political and moral crisis of our people but also a theological crisis of our faith. The incomprehensible thing about 'Auschwitz' for us was not the executioners and their helpers, nor even the technical perfection of the mass extermination and the hiddenness of God. For us it was the silence of people who watched or looked away or closed their eyes in order to deliver the victims alone and forsaken to mass murder. For us 'Auschwitz' became not only a question about the meaning of suffering, as it did for the Jews, but also the question of power to live with such a burden of guilt and shame and mourning. 'After Auschwitz there are no more poems,' declared T.W.Adorno at that time. Can one still talk of God 'after Auschwitz'? Is theology still possible 'after Auschwitz'? We replied, 'Yes', but only because there had been a theology in Auschwitz. Only in making present the prayers which were prayed in the gas chambers, the Shema Israel and the Lord's Prayer, can we again pray to God today. Only in thinking of the victims do we find courage for life and hope for another future.

We began on the basis of this insight to ask the Christian and theological traditions in Germany: Why did Christians and churches, with few exceptions, on the whole keep silent? There was no lack of personal courage. We found the following patterns of behaviour and prejudices in the tradition:

(a) 'Faith is a private matter': faith is to do with saving the soul and the inner peace of the conscience, and not with politics. The privatization of religion in the bourgeois world of the nineteenth-century secularized politics and handed over public life to other powers. This gave rise to the modern division of human life into public life on the one hand and private life on the other, into a political power politics without morality on the one hand and a personal morality without power on the other. Many Christians who abhorred Hitler and bewailed the fate of the Jews went on so-called 'emigration inwards': they attempted to save their souls inwardly and outwardly adapted to political demands. They did not save their personal innocence. They were guilty towards their Jewish fellow-citizens because they kept silent when they should have spoken.

Modern theologians with their transcendental, existentialist or personalistic orientation simply reflected this modern split in consciousness. They came to grief on the demands of that time and 'after Auschwitz' are no longer relevant. The political theology which we developed against them starts from public testimony and public reponsibility for faith and is a theology which is emphatically critical of society and power. The gospel of Christ is not about a private person; it is a public proclamation. The salvation of Christ is not private salvation but the salvation of the world. Therefore it comes into deadly conflict with the godless powers of its time. Christian faith is personal conviction, however: not a private matter, but public testimony to the justice and peace of God in this violent world.

(b) The separation of religion and politics: since the Reformation, the Protestant 'two kingdoms doctrine' has taught the difference between church and state, religion and politics. From that follows the claim that the church must be unpolitical and politics unreligious. When Hitler came to power, the churches did not feel responsible for the human dignity and human rights of the Communists, Socialists, Democrats and Jews who were the first to be persecuted. Only when Hitler wanted to subjugate the churches was there resistance from the church. Apart from individuals like Dietrich Bonhoeffer there was no political resistance from Christians and the churches. 'The church must remain the church,' it was said, no matter what happens in state and society. With this attitude the churches became guilty of 'Auschwitz'. Modern 'church theologies' reflect this separation of religion and politics. Just as a church cannot exist 'unpolitically' within a society, so a theology cannot just be a theology of the church apart from politics. There are indeed theologians who are unaware of politics, but in principle there are no apolitical theologians. Churches and theologies which claim to be 'unpolitical' always co-operate with the powers of the *status quo* and have always entered into conservative alliances. Their alleged political neutrality is the price of their privileges. The new political theology does not want to 'politicize' the churches, but to make the churches aware of their political ties and 'Christianize' their political existence. The church is an institution with the freedom to criticize society (Johann-Baptist Metz). For in the end every church which appeals to Christ must be reminded that Christ was not sacrificed on the altar by a priest between two candles but was crucified by the Roman occupation forces between two Jewish freedom fighters at Golgotha, 'outside the city'.

(*c*) The privatization of faith and the separation of the church from politics has had a fateful efect on the public life of society and politics. In Germany it gave rise to what has been called 'Realpolitik', i.e. naked power politics without a conscience or moral scruple. 'One cannot rule the state by the Sermon on the Mount,' said Chancellor Bismarck, though he himself was very devout. This German Realpolitik set off two world wars and over a long period destroyed our people physically and spiritually, though in the short term it seemed to be quite successful. By contrast it is not only more responsible but also wiser to orientate politics by the criteria of human rights and to regard all national politics as a moral task on behalf of humankind. Morality and religion, conscience and responsibility will have to come back into politics 'after Auschwitz' if humankind is to be saved from a nuclear holocaust.

The political theology which we began in Germany in the 1960s became a theological movement extending far beyond the boundaries of Western Europe. At a very early stage there was a reciprocal exchange with theology in Latin America, first with the 'theology of revolution' and then with the 'theology of liberation'. At an equally early stage there were contacts with the civil rights movement and 'Black Theology' in the USA. At a later stage there was also an exchange with Minjung theology in Korea and other contextual theologies in Third World countries. Similar political theologies are coming into being everywhere today from Christians who are devoting themselves to liberation, social justice and human rights in a specific political context.

The peace movement has been growing in both German states because of political disappointments. It reached its highpoint in 1981 and 1982 with enormous mass demonstrations and human chains extending over hundreds of miles. It strengthened the discussion over peace which had already been carried on in our churches since the rearmament of West Germany and led to the Protestant Church in the German Democratic Republic issuing a 'rejection' of the 'spirit of logic and the praxis of the system of nuclear deterrence' which was as solemn as it was binding. In 1982 the Reformed Church in West Germany regarded this system of deterrence as 'incompatible' with Christian faith and called for a *status confessionis*. The Protestant Church in West Germany and the Catholic conferences of bishops reacted with rather more restraint, because they recognized the system of military deterrence as a form of securing peace which was 'still possible' by way of political security. However, this argument is losing its force as year by year all that happens is further rearmament.

In its history the Christian church has developed various concepts for dealing with the power which can lead to war: the doctrine of the just war and the pacifist ethics of discipleship. According to the traditional doctrine of the just war, no war waged with the means of mass annihilation can be called 'just'. A war of the end-time waged with nuclear weapons goes beyond this scheme because such a war is not provided for in the doctrine. So there is a dispute as to whether the doctrine of the just war can still apply. The discussion has rightly concentrated on 'peace through justice' or a new doctrine of 'just peace', as has been commended by the document from the United Methodist Council of Bishops in the United States (1986). The pacifist ethics of discipleship has so far been practised by the traditional pacifist churches and individual Christian groups. It is regarded as the mark of true Christians who have parted company with this evil, violent world. In the nuclear end-time, in which we have been existing since Hiroshima, this gospel ethics of peace is no longer to be practised just in a small group but also universally and politically, because it is not only moral, but also the only rational approach. Since the middle of the 1970s, the political theology which we began in the 1960s in the awareness of the Jewish holocaust in Auschwitz has increasingly become a theology of peace in the face of the nuclear holocaust which threatens all mankind.[9]

4. Atomic end-time and apocalyptic hope

The expression 'end-time' was traditionally used for the apocalyptic conceptions of those events which took place at the end of this world as 'the last things' and represented the birth pangs of God's new world. In 1959 Günter Anders was one of the first to speak of a 'nuclear theology', a 'nuclear apocalypse' and an 'end-time' without hope.[10] I shall compare his theses with the Jewish and Christian traditions of apocalyptic hope.

1. 'Nuclear theology' interprets nuclear power with theological and apocalyptic concepts because this power goes beyond all traditional political concepts. The country which becomes a nuclear power has taken a leap into the absolute. It has gained omnipotence, if only by being able to threaten the destruction of the world. At the same time it decides whether humankind will or will not be. This nuclear situation is the end of politics. No political or military demarcations are possible any longer. In so far as 'the infernal' belongs in theology, Günter Anders thought that there was no step of the nuclear powers which did not go over to a theological sphere. The nuclear inferno

which they threaten to unleash can only be understood in the images of apocalyptic terror.

To this early analysis by Anders it should be added that there is evidently also something religious about a nuclear power in that it represents a *mysterium fascinosum et tremendum*. The worship of the power of annihilation is certainly the supreme blasphemy. The system of global nuclear deterrence contains within itself the suicidal religious tendencies of nihilism. Therefore the system of nuclear deterrence is not just a question of military, political or ethical assessment but a supremely religious question which challenges Christian faith to make a confession.

2. Günter Anders thought that the general 'blindness to apocalyptic' hindered the realistic perception of this endtime situation, and that the universal 'dullness of apocalypse' paralysed the will to survive.[11] That is true of the official playing down of the nuclear threat. But there is also a perceptible weariness of apocalypse. That is the paralysis which arises out of the analysis of our helplessness in the face of overwhelming nuclear power.

3. After his attempt to understand the nuclear age with apocalyptic pictures, by 1960 Günter Anders had begun to doubt whether apocalypse was the right expression for the nuclear threat. In 1960 he found the following differences: nuclear apocalyptic knows only the 'naked apocalypse', the 'apocalypse without kingdom'. Here was a reversal of the nineteenth-century belief in progress, which hoped for a 'kingdom without apocalypse'. There were no grounds for the Christian expectation of the end in its day, but there were grounds for seeing our day as the nuclear end-time. The Christian expectation was directed to God's judgment on human guilt, but the nuclear expectation of the end points to human failure *and* human death. In Christian terms that means that 'the future has already begun'; in nuclear terms that must mean: 'The time of no future has now begun.'[12]

But the difference goes considerably further: any interpretation of the problems of the present time in apocalyptic categories foists human responsibility off on God and is deeply irresponsible and immoral. The threat of a nuclear end is called an 'Armageddon' in order to foist the blame for the crime against humanity on God. The imagery of the apocalypse is used in order to make the crime a fate, since it makes one an accomplice to the one who commits this crime. A way out of the catastrophe is sought in apocalyptic imagery and is found in the 'rapture' of the believers before the 'great tribulation'. This escapism is the abandonment of any responsibility for the earth and for one's children. Revelation 16.16 says of the biblical 'Armageddon' that *God* will assemble the spirits of the devil at the place of Armageddon for the 'great day of God'. What does the last day of humanity in the nuclear end, released by human beings, have to do with this 'great day of God'? To put it quite simply: nothing at all!

'Apocalypse' means revelation, and in the biblical tradition it denotes the manifestation of men and women before God and of God before men and women in God's judgment and kingdom. It has nothing to do with the fear of catastrophes and belief in fate; it formulates hope for God in the final danger to the world. The great anxiety of the apocalyptists is not the destruction of this old world of injustice and violence, but the withdrawal of God from creation because God might 'repent of' having created the world.[13] The recollection of the story of Noah and the flood underlies all biblical apocalypses relating to the end of the world, and this recollection arouses the hope that God will remain true to his decision over creation. The apocalyptists are not Cassandras who always count on the worst in order to be right if it happens, and to rejoice if it does not. They establish hope in danger since they see through the horizon of the end of the world into the coming new world of God.

5. The nuclear catastrophe: where is God?

Meditation on this question does not bring an answer, but only deepens the question so that it becomes outcry and lament. I would like to turn the answers that we have already given ourselves, with or without a religious consciousness, as to how we may continue to live as we have been doing, and not have to change, into God's questions which deeply unsettle us and make us search for new answers. In the light of a possible nuclear catastrophe, not only do we human beings need God, but God needs us! That is the theological question that we have to put to ourselves.

One cannot avoid the impression that theology has not yet become aware of the whole significance of the new situation. Like American theology, German theology has only reluctantly and hesitantly addressed the nuclear end-time of the human race, and hitherto has done so only on ethical and political grounds. The statements by the Reformed Alliance (1981) and the Evangelical Church of Germany (1982), the memoranda of the Roman Catholic bishops and the Methodist bishops in the USA, the declarations by other denominations and the public discussion on nuclear weapons clearly show a limited perception of the situation. So far we have not adequately understood theologically either the religious challenge of 'nuclearism' or the eschatological dimension of the system of nuclear deterrence. Only on the periphery and in more spontaneous comments are God and the nuclear catastrophe brought together. With respect to the refutation of God by the nuclear holocaust which is possible at any time, the 'God after Auschwitz' discussion returns on another level with the whole of humanity and life on this earth which will burn in the nuclear firestorm, and lose all ability to live in the subsequent nuclear winter.

In that case, where is God? First I shall bring together some theological answers and discuss them in the forum of God's judgment.

1. God is the almighty. God affects everything everywhere.

God therefore also brings about the nuclear catastrophe. We do not know why, but we must bow to his incomprehensible will. – Such an interpretation will not bring about trust in God, which is its purpose, but rather hatred of God. God is made guilty for human crimes. In that case it is no longer possible to distinguish between God and Satan. That is not just irresponsible, but also intolerable as a way of excusing human beings before God's judgment.

Behind this, however, is the deeper theological problem which is recognized in the Auschwitz discussion by both Jews and Christians: God cannot be termed 'the almighty' in an absolute sense and seen as the cause of everything that happens in this world.[14] What is almighty is God's essential love which 'bears all things, endures all things, believes all things and hopes all things' (I Cor.13.7). He is not God as the 'almighty' but as the one who loves unconditionally. So his 'omnipotence' is to be understood in terms of eternal love as universal tolerance, as his boundless capacity for suffering, with which he supports his creation on earth despite all contradictions and in so doing remains faithful to it. God has hope for this world, and so he waits for it and keeps its future open.

2. God will not allow the nuclear catastrophe. God keeps to his covenant with Noah by which he has guaranteed life on this earth and promised that no new 'flood' will come. This theological understanding also puts trust in God in place of the human responsibility which must be accepted because human beings have gained this power to annihilate the world and will not give it up again. It is childish and irresponsible to think that God would limit human freedom where this freedom becomes life-threatening and deadly. This religious illusion can already been seen to be illusion by the way in which it has been bloodily disappointed so that people have turned desperately to God with the question 'How can you allow it?' – Verdun and Stalingrad, Auschwitz and Hiroshima. This theological expedient, too, encourages human irresponsibility – 'God allowed it' – and as an excuse in God's judgment it is

intolerable. The God who 'allows' such cruel human crimes as an accomplice can hardly be called 'God'.

3. God will save believers from the coming nuclear catastrophe. After the shorter first tribulation and before the longer second tribulation, true believers will be 'caught up' into the clouds to meet the returning Christ (I Thess.4.13-18). Unbelievers will perish in the nuclear catastrophe. The coming Christ will then build his thousand-year-kingdom on earth with believers. This escapism of apocalyptic fantasy not only encourages irresponsibility about nuclear crimes against humanity but even justifies them indirectly. Christians who are certain of their 'rapture' allow the world to go to hell. They no longer know the love of Christ. When the judge of the world asks them about their acts of mercy, they will have no answer. Their fate has been described clearly enough in Matthew 25.

4. The nuclear catastrophe of humankind and all life on earth is also a catastrophic experience for God himself. If the creation is destroyed, what becomes of its creator? If humanity, the image of God, is obliterated, who is God? A God without earthly creation, a God without his image in his creation? All Christian creeds acknowlege that in Christ God has become human. What does this incarnation of God mean if there are no more human beings? Christ died for the reconciliation of all men and women with God. If there are no longer any men and women, has Christ then died in vain? One answer which comes out of the discussion of Auschwitz points to God's suffering. In his Shekinah, his indwelling in the people of his choice, in his name which he has hallowed through his people, God himself participates in the suffering of his people and the humiliation of his honour. God himself was *in* Auschwitz. He suffered with those who suffocated in the gas chambers. Their suffering was his suffering and their tears were his tears. He is the companion in the suffering of his people.[15] So even now he could be the companion of his people in suffering in the nuclear holocaust which is possible at any time. In God's 'indwelling', God's spirit immanent in the world, God would

34

then himself suffer the nuclear catastrophe, and even if humanity fell dumb, there would remain the 'inexpressible sighing' of the divine Spirit. In that case it would not just be a catastrophe for God's world, but also a catastrophic experience for God. When the nuclear catastrophe takes place, God weeps over his lost creation and his annihilated humanity in infinite, divine grief. But to the degree to which God takes upon himself the unutterable suffering of this catastrophe of humankind and suffers in it himself, he also shows the faith which he keeps with his creation. He will not hinder us, but through his own suffering he will bring this annihilated world into the creation of his new world. – Belief in the God who suffers with us brings communion with God to those who have been abandoned by God and gives them consolation in their hopeless suffering.[16] Where this communion with God is experienced in suffering, there hope is also preserved or born again that at the end God will still be victor over all human crimes and 'wash away all tears from their eyes' (Rev.21.4). This is my personal experience of God and the ground of my hope. I find it expressed very movingly in a hymn by W.H.Vanstone:

> Thou art God, no monarch thou,
> thron'd in easy state to reign.
> Thou art God, whose arms of love
> aching, spent, the world sustain.[17]

5. Finally, the nuclear catastrophe is also the catastrophe of God himself in as much as God lives by virtue of his love wholly in his relationship to the creation and to humankind. Therefore the annihilation of humankind is also the annihilation of the God who has become human and the annihilation of all life on this earth is also the annihilation of the living God himself. Dorothee Sölle has emphasized this relationship most strongly: 'No generation in previous history could say no to the creation the way that we can. No previous generation was in a position not only to crucify Christ again and again but also to abolish God himself, the Creator, the Being in relationship. We might

seek to console ourselves with the superficial Christian way of talking about the "eternal God" – but that would be self-deception, because after the final solution of the nuclear holocaust there is neither father nor mother in heaven nor any longer a creator.'[18] Anxiety over nuclear catastrophe is, moreover, anxiety about God. That gives this anxiety an infinite theological depth which no simple trust in the eternal, unassailable and uninvolved God can suppress or assuage. However, we must also see the other side. Does this not also mean that God is handed over to those who commit crimes against humanity? Who will then bring the criminals to account and bring justice to their victims? In the 'God after Auschwitz' discussion, Richard Rubenstein spoke of the 'death of God' in Auschwitz.[19] Emil Fackenheim challenged him: if Hitler had also killed God along with the Jews, who would bring Hitler to book? If Jews gave up their belief in God after Auschwitz and stopped existing as Israel, then they would give Hitler a posthumous victory.[20]

The crimes and terrors of Auschwitz have certainly revived the old protest atheism. 'Creator, creation and creature are refuted through Auschwitz,' wrote Rolf Hochhuth in *The Representative*.[21] But they have also called forth a new protest theism: 'Theology is... an expression of the longing that the murderer should not triumph over the innocent victim,'[22] declared Max Horkheimer, one of the fathers of the critical philosophy of the 'Frankfurt school'. The longing for justice and faith in the one who finally guarantees it is a stronger potential for protest against the preparation and threat of nuclear mass annihilation than the old protest atheism. But the two are mutually supplementary: protest atheism rules out false religious consolation and irresponsible religious expedients. Protest theism sets possible crimes against humanity and all those who allow them by their passivity and indifference in the light of the divine judgment. God is the judge of the murderers and the avenger of the victims. The nuclear catastrophe will not annihilate this apocalyptic horizon of the last judgment but rather lead humankind directly into it.

6. Hope against danger

Those who feel threatened often react suicidally. They become paralysed like the rabbit facing the snake; they strike the guilty with violence; they consume themselves. These reactions are widespread today. There is an increase in resignation: 'But we can't do anything.' There is an increase in hatred: a search for scapegoats in the hostile 'evil kingdom'. There is an increase in cynicism: 'After us the flood.' There are increasing religious attempts to foist the responsibility on God and make him responsible for the crimes of humanity. In such reactions men and women lose the courage to live and give up protest along with the courage to live. Where do we find the strength to affirm life in the face of the threat and the passion to do what we need to do today, before it is too late?

Christian hope is not directed towards a happy end in world history. False comfort is just as dangerous as general despair. However, Jewish and Christian hope knows a 'hermeneutics of danger', of which Walter Benjamin said: 'It means to take possession of a memory which flashes out in the moment of danger.'[23] At a moment of deadly danger the biblical stories of God are expressive and arouse hope where otherwise there is nothing to hope for. The memories of being delivered from distress do not deny the danger. But they speak of the God who has made the hopeless distress of the people his own and has led his people out of it. The recollection of these experiences of God leads us to learn to 'see through the horizon', as the Indonesian word for hope puts it. The Christian recollection makes present the suffering and death of Christ as he was abandoned by God, and through the anticipation of his resurrection from the dead arouses hope for the victory of life against the power of death. This recollection of Christ's experience of God leads us to see through the horizon of the threat of nuclear catastrophe to the kingdom of justice and life. Anyone who perceives this horizon of God in the threat of the destruction of the world is even now beginning to live and act in accordance with it.

From this there follows first the acceptance of one's own situation in the nuclear end-time of humankind and secondly the acceptance of responsibility for the life of the coming generations in this situation. The yes to life in the face of total danger leads to unconditional protest against annihilation and the threat of annihilation. A nuclear war in this generation is possible and therefore is to be feared. This commits us to 'say no to the spirit, logic and praxis of the system of nuclear deterrence', as the Protestant churches in the German Democratic Republic put it, and to work for a world community in peace on the basis of justice. Only the reduction of violence and the threat of violence will lead to this future.

Hope against danger leads to paradoxical action, i.e. action against appearances and against prospects of success, because by virtue of hope in God one sees more than the eye rightly sees, when it looks into the future of the world. There is no theological meaning to Auschwitz, but only protest against the crime which is theologically grounded in God's judgment. There is no apocalyptic meaning to the nuclear annihilation of the world but only the protest of the apocalyptic hope for God against all the powers which make possible and prepare for that annihilation of the world.

7. Justice, not security, creates peace

The biblical traditions and the Christian experience of faith say clearly that only justice creates a lasting peace (*shalom*). So there is no way to peace other than through just action and a concern for justice world-wide. All Christian memoranda have rightly taken this view. But what is 'justice'?

Jews and Christians will start out from their experience of

God's justice if they want to bring justice into the world. They experience God's justice as creative, justifying and itself creating justice. God is just because he brings justice to unjust men and puts unjust men and women right. His justice is a saving justice. Therefore one can pray with Psalm 31.2: 'Save me through your justice.' Psalm 146.7 confesses that God 'executes justice for those who suffer violence'. Through this justice God creates that peace which lasts: *shalom*.

It follows from this that there is no peace where injustice and violence reign, even if 'law and order' is enforced there. Peace does not bring justice, but justice brings peace. Injustice always creates inequalities and destroys balances. Unjust systems can be kept alive only through violence. Where there is violence there is no peace, for where violence reigns it is death that reigns and not life.

I shall now relate this Jewish-Christian concept of justice to the concepts of justice in our legal system.

1. An earlier concept of European jurisprudence defined justice as *justitia distributiva: suum cuique* – to each his own. This brilliant formula combines equality in the eyes of the law with the real difference between human beings. To each according his or her capacity and in accordance with his or her needs (Marx), or as the Hutterite brethren say: 'Everyone gives whatever he can and gets whatever he needs.' However, this concept of justice is primarily related to objects, to achievements and goods: all men and women have a right to life, food, work and freedom.

2. The personal concept of judgment, through which human society is brought about, goes beyond this concept of justice which is related to objects. The personal concept consists in the reciprocal recognition and acceptance of other people. Reciprocal recognition of human status and mutual acceptance creates a humane and just community. That is in accordance with Christian experiences: 'Accept one another, as Christ has accepted you, for the glory of God' (Rom.15.17). This personal

concept of justice also underlies the modern federalist concepts of democratic society like covenant and constitution.

3. But the supreme form of justice is the law of mercy, through which those who are without rights receive justice. This is the justice of the 'God of widows and orphans'. In this world of human injustice and human violence, the divine justice takes on the structure of the 'preferential option for the poor', as the Latin American liberation theologians put it. That does not mean that 'grace goes before justice', but that those deprived of their rights get their rights, and that the unjust are converted to justice. This divine justice does not stand outside the human legal order but is itself the justice-creating source of that legal order which leads to lasting peace. Like the recognition of the human dignity of others, so too the creation and protection of the right of the poor, weak and sick is the foundation for any lasting human system of justice.

8. The way to lasting peace

The biblical traditions and the Jewish and Christian experience of faith speak of a comprehensive peace because they are speaking of God's peace. Shalom means the sanctification of the whole of life that God has made, in all its relationships. It is blessed life in communion with the lifegiving God, with other human beings and with all other creatures: peace with God, peace among human beings, peace with nature. For God's sake *shalom* cannot be limited to religions or individuals. By its tendency *shalom* is universal and lasting. What Jews and Christians experience of it in history, however, are also beginnings and anticipations of that peace of God which one day will bring all creatures to eternal life. Judaism and Christianity are movements of concrete hope of peace for all peoples and all creatures.

It follows from this that peace in history is not a state of affairs but a process; not a possession of our own but a shared way. Peace is not the absence of violence but the presence of justice.

In peace research, a distinction is made between a negative and a positive definition of peace.[24] The negative definition says that peace is not war and is thus the absence of the use of military force, of anxiety and oppression. This negative understanding of peace is present when it is said that the system of nuclear deterrence has 'kept the peace' for the last forty years. Quite apart from the fact that this is not true in the case of all people, this confuses peace with a cease-fire, and the costs of the system of nuclear deterrence are concealed. Certainly it is easy to agree on a negative definition, but it is not enough.

The positive definition of peace calls peace a state of social justice, the democratic settlement of conflict and equilibrium in a permanent development of all. Some regard this as a utopia, but even the negative concept of peace cannot function without these positive elements.

The Christian concept of peace combines the two definitions, but it gives priority to the positive definition of peace by stressing justice. It follows from this that peace in history is a shared way on which there are both steps forward and steps back. This way is concerned with a reduction of armaments and force and the building up of trust and community.

There is never lasting peace in history just for the present generation; it arises out of responsibility for justice between the generations. Humanity is created as a series of generations. Therefore every generation is indebted to past generations, and every generation is responsible for the life of coming generations. Only justice in this unwritten contract between the human generations promotes a lasting peace. Therefore peace in history is never a state with which one can be content, but is always a way one must take in order to create time for humankind and make possible the life of generations to come.

In view of the contradictions of modern society, there is now public discussion of the Sermon on the Mount, discussion

41

which is particularly concerned with freedom from violence and the overcoming of enmity.

This presupposes that the original sin which leads people into death does not lie in eating the forbidden fruit in paradise, as Genesis 3 tells us, but in the act of violence which is reported in the story of Cain and Abel. Only through Augustine did the doctrine of original sin enter the theological tradition of the West. The Jews do not know it, although they read the same texts. Nor do Orthodox theologians have a doctrine of inherited guilt, but only a doctrine of inherited weakness.

According to the Priestly creation story sin begins with the extension of acts of violence over the earth: 'The earth was full of evil' (Gen.6.13). The 'violent in the world' are those who are evil. These are the tyrannical rulers of the world, who allow themselves to be worshipped as 'sons of God'. But violent rule is against God and against his love for his creatures. Violent rule does not serve life, but chaos and death. Therefore God brings the flood over the earth. Only Noah 'led a godly life in his time' (6.9) and is saved and becomes the ancestor of the new humankind.

Recollection of this story underlies the Sermon on the Mount. The Messiah who expresses God's wisdom brings peace and overcomes acts of violence. Not only evil but also the law of the retribution of evil with evil; not only acts of violence but also the limitation of them by violent resistance are done away with. Non-violent action and the repayment of evil with good are the hallmarks of the messianic world. Only the justice which consists in creative love brings lasting peace into the world.

9. Taking responsibility for the enemy

According to the Sermon on the Mount, 'love of the enemy' is the perfect form of love of neighbour which accords with good and thus with justice. It is the way to lasting peace on earth. Anyone who gets involved in a dispute and has a conflict always becomes subject to the law of retribution: an eye for an eye and a tooth for tooth. Anyone who accepts this law of retribution towards the enemy gets involved in a vicious circle from which there is no escape: one must become one's enemy's enemy and is caught up into this enmity. If evil is recompensed with evil, then the one evil is always orientated on the other evil, because only in that way is it justified. In former times one could survive with one eye and the loss of a few teeth. In the nuclear age the arms race, which works in the same way, and the threat of 'massive retribution', lead the world to universal death. There is liberation for life only when orientation on the enemy ceases and deterrence by the threat of retribution no longer rules. The attitude to one's enemy with which Christ replaces deterrence is 'love of the enemy' (Matt.5.43ff.). What does that mean in the conditions of the nuclear age?

Love of the enemy is not retributive love, but creative love. Anyone who repays evil with good is no longer reacting, but creating something new. The love of one's enemy presupposes great sovereignty towards one's enemy. The freer one becomes of anxiety about one's enemy, the better love of the enemy will succeed. But love of the enemy can never mean subjection to the enemy and confirmation of his enmity, for in that case there would be no one left who could love the enemy. On the contrary, it is the creative and intelligent overcoming of enmity. In love of the enemy one is no longer asking 'How can I protect myself against the enemy and attack possible enmity?', but 'How can I remove the enemy's enmity?' By loving the enemy we make the enemy part of our own responsibility. We learn to see ourselves and recognize ourselves through the eyes of others. Therefore love of the enemy is not an expression of abstract good intentions, 'dispositional ethics', as Max Weber put it, but 'ethics of responsibility'.[25] Love of the enemy is certainly difficult in private life. But in the nuclear age it is politically the only reasonable course, because nowadays we cannot secure our peace by eliminating all our possible enemies

43

or threatening them with extermination – where would we stop? We can do so only by dismantling our enmities and taking responsibility for common security and a lasting development. Politics in this first common age of humanity requires us to think for one another and calls for a great deal of empathy. The first question is not how Western Europe can protect itself against the 'Russian threat' but how we can arrive at a common order of peace in both Western and Eastern Europe. We must demilitarize public awareness and political thinking and transfer the way in which we deal with our opponents in a democracy to the way in which we deal with 'enemies' internationally. To justify German power politics Bismarck once remarked that 'One cannot rule a state by the Sermon on the Mount'. Instead he promised the Germans 'iron and tears'. We have inflicted and got back both to excess in two world wars. Nothing has been left but unforgettable sorrow and intolerable guilt. I would claim that no politics of survival in the nuclear age can go against the Sermon on the Mount. One can 'do politics' with the Sermon on the Mount, but only the politics of peace.

10. Overcoming violence with non-violence

From the politics of loving one's enemy there follows the politics of overcoming the rule of violence by non-violence. 'Non-violence' does not mean the depoliticizing and renunciation of power, because we have to distinguish between 'power' and 'violence'. By power I mean the just use of force. By violence I mean the unjust use of power. In this sense the modern state has the monopoly of violence in society, and we speak of naked power, brutality and tyranny where force is used illegally, illegitimately and in a way which goes against human rights. Christianity has not been able to abolish the 'culture of force' in our societies. However, it has made it necessary to justify every response of force, especially the state use of force. It has broken with the 'innocence of the beast' which Nietzsche worshipped. The law also puts limits on the state monopoly of force, not only in domestic politics towards the citizens of one's own state, but also in foreign politics towards other states and humankind. To threaten humankind with a nuclear holocaust is a brutal act of force which nothing can justify. The threat and use of nuclear weapons and other means of mass annihilation exceed the right of any state.

The first form of overcoming violence is to tie every exercise of power to the law. From that follows the duty of resistance to any unjust use of power, whether this is illegal, illegitimate or directed against human rights. The principle of 'non-violence' does not exclude the struggle for power when this struggle is involved in binding power to justice. Anyone who joins the resistance in a manifestly violent regime is only doing his or her duty as a citizen, when he or she stands for the restoration of the law or for the rights of the oppressed.

The power of the peoples who suffer under a violent regime is not terrorism but solidarity. Terrorism disqualifies the goals of the liberation and justifies only the rule of violence. The mass solidarity of the people and the peoples deprives the rule of force of that semblance of justice and robs its threats of their terror. We have recently had a series of examples of peoples overcoming military dictatorships by bloodless revolutions: in Portugal, Spain, Greece, Argentina, the Philippines. Violent rule has a weak footing when it is rejected from within the people and is also isolated in foreign affairs by other peoples, and so is beyond both anxiety and trust.

It is possible to overcome violence non-violently. But it can also call for martyrdom. We think of Gandhi and Martin Luther King Jr. We think above all of Christ himself. When we think of them, we discover that it is not just active action which has liberating power and leads to 'success'; suffering, too, has liberating power, and this can work even more convincingly in the long term.

11. The categorical imperative of life in the nuclear age

The nuclear age is the first common age for all peoples and nations. The nuclear threat has made all men and women together candidates for death. The rapidly developing ecological crisis of the global environment has confronted all nations – each in its own way, but nevertheless all together – with the same task. Particularist thought which is directed against other people and nations and which fails to note the universal community of threat and tasks is not only morally reprehensible but also irrational and fatal. The possibility of life on earth depends on how quickly and thoroughly we recognize that we are neighbours on a vulnerable planet and that we have to care for one another and for our descendants. All more recent 'State of the World Reports' indicate that the common world of the earth is in great danger and that humanity is not in very good shape. We need a convincing ethics of the common life. Lenin himself said that: 'Situations may arise in which the interest of all humankind must be accorded priority over the class interests of the proletariat.' That is also true of the 'Western world'.

The present crises have arisen out of competition and a power struggle: everyone attempting to win at the cost of the others. The starting point was the assumption that in the battle for existence 'the fittest' survives. Nowadays this principle is likely to be the death of both weak and strong and is destroying the future of the earth. The principle of life is that respect for the interests of others is the presupposition for the perception of the interests of all, and only a mutual guarantee of security can guarantee the security of all.[26] National selfishness, class rule and enrichment at the cost of others are reprehensible because they are fatal. Humanity and the earth can no longer afford this power struggle and competition. The first question in all great political and economic decisions must therefore be: does it or does it not serve the common life of humankind?

An ethics for humankind has become a task for humankind; it must therefore be freed from the particular national, economic and cultural interests by which ethics was previously dominated. The ethical values of life, life together and the survival of the earth have become absolute values over against any purely particular interests.

The separation of politics, economics, law and the sciences from ethics has become intolerable and can no longer be tolerated. The sorry experience of our present crises is a convincing demonstration that economics, politics and the sciences perish without an ethical orientation.

The common formulation of a categorical imperative is necessary for the life of humankind on this earth so that the great problems of humankind today can be resolved in a responsible way. It is also time for people to detach themselves from their particular interests and reflect on the 'eternal truths' which form the foundation of their common humanity, and subject all that is theirs to these truths. The nuclear age has become the first age of humankind. If it is not to become the last, we must think in terms of humankind in all questions. The categorical imperative for the survival of humankind runs:

> So act that the maxims of your action through your will become a universal law for all men and women and the universal law for all men and women becomes the maxim of your actions.

12. Are Christian capable of peace?

How can Christians, how can communities and how can churches organize their task for peace through justice?

The church exists in a variety of social forms. Here I mention them from the top downwards: 1. the universal church; 2. the territorial church: 3. the local community; 4. the voluntary group and the movement. The service of peace must take different forms on these different levels. In my view it is worth making a distinction here so that no one level takes on too much.

I shall begin from the bottom with the voluntary group.

1. Commitment to peace always calls for personal commitment to non-violent action and personal readiness for sacrifice. Therefore peace groups and 'Third World' groups for social justice are springing up everywhere. Here people who are involved meet voluntarily and work on a specific task which they recognize in common as their own task and adopt it. They develop their own readiness for involvement in demonstrations and social action. A new spirituality also comes into being along with this new readiness for public action: Dietrich Bonhoeffer called this new life-style 'Resistance and Surrender' (this is the title of the German edition of his *Letters and Papers from Prison*); in Taizé it is called 'Contemplation and Struggle'. In the Latin American basic communities one comes across 'mysticism and liberation'.

These peace groups form regional and international networks and so build up an 'ecumene from below'. But they are groups and movements and networks of like-minded people. So the Catholic peace movement Pax Christi has a problem with the hierarchy of the Catholic Church in the Federal Republic of Germany. So the base communities in Latin America are not appreciated by all bishops. So the Christian peace movement in the Protestant church in Germany is looked on with great mistrust. The reason for this is not just the anxiety of the representatives of institutions at the uncontrollable spontaneity of these groups and movements, but also the fact that the local church communities do not consist only of those with like minds but also of those who think differently. Here the 'Association of Catholic Soldiers' in the Federal Republic of Germany issues polemic against Pax Christi and the Protestant army chaplains fight the Protestant peace movement in our church. So what can one expect of the local community? What can one suggest to it?

2. The local community comes into being from the proclamation of the gospel, the celebration of the eucharist and baptism. It usually gathers on Sunday morning for worship.

People meet together who have differing ideas about peace and justice. They do not come to meet those of a like mind in political questions. Therefore the local church community can hardly become a peace group. In my view its testimony to peace lies, rather, on a different level: so far the local community has been predominantly a religious community and a worshipping community. But if it hears the whole gospel of Christ it will be transformed into a community of life. The more Christians live together in the local community, the more they will perceive the social, economic and political conflicts in which they exist and ask about justice and peace in these conflicts. The more they recognize that the salvation of God means the total wholeness of the creation, the more they will perceive their own tasks in the healing of the social and political diseases of the society in which they live. Alongside worship it will then be important for the community to meet together in plenary session where working groups give their reports and local tasks are discussed. It is also the place where the peace groups can introduce their experiences to the local community in order to set the learning process of peace in motion there.

3. The territorial churches are neither local communities nor peace movements. Their context is the region in which the territory lies. They must take up the conflicts which are prevalent there and attempt in regional peace conferences to replace mutual assured destruction with mutual responsibility. For divided Europe there is the 'European Churches Conference'. As its political counterpart there are the conferences on European security, for the development of 'measures for building up trust' and mutual security partnerships between Western and Eastern European nations.

Finally, the universal church has so far become visible only at a confessional level: in Rome, in Geneva, in the World Federations or Alliances of the various denominations. It could become visible if that pan-Christian convocation for peace comes into being at which Christianity as whole bears witness unequivocally and with the seriousness of self-commitment before a universe threatened with death to the justice of God, the peace of the nations and the life of the creation.

4. The motto for all forms of organization in the church is: 'Think globally – act locally.' If this is to be possible, communications in the churches must be improved. On the whole the pastoral letters, encyclicals and memoranda on peace that we have had so far have come along a one-way street from the top down. They have seldom got to the bottom, nor are they really taken seriously. Conversely, the reports of experience from the grass roots are seldom read and noted 'up there'. So it seems to me to be the task of church governments to note the experiences and questions of the grass roots and to hand them on. Only if the churches at all levels, in territorial churches, local communities and peace groups, come together in a joint learning process for justice and peace, can they speak with one voice – and then they will be heard.

III

The Ecological Situation: The Theology and Ethics of Creation

1. The ecological crisis of modern civilization

According to a recent investigation in Saarbrücken, West Germany, the incidence of lung cancer is increasing there, in a region where the trees are becoming diseased and dying. The trees are becoming diseased and dying because waste gases from industry, traffic and houses are poisoning the air and acid rain is falling on the forests and destroying plants and animals. There is a vicious circle of death which runs from human society to the natural environment and from the death of trees rebounds on human beings. The human creation of modern industrial society is leading to the exhaustion of nature. The reckless exploitation of natural resources is destroying the natural foundations of life. There have also been earlier environmental catastrophes. But in earlier times, after the catastrophes nature could restore life and the multiplicity of living beings. Now, though, whole species of animals and plants are dying out, and no one will be able to bring them back again. Will our children one day have to experience spring without butterflies, summer without bird-song and autumn without apples?

This creeping crisis, which is spreading imperceptibly, is called 'environmental pollution' or 'ecological crisis'. People act as though only nature outside – the Black Forest or the

Rhine or the air over the Ruhr – were affected by it. But to think that way is to play down the situation criminally. In reality this is a crisis of our whole 'scientific and technological civilization'. The project of industrial society has run into a dead end. Unless there is a radical change in the fundamental orientations of our society; unless we succeed in finding an alternative life-style for dealing with nature and ourselves, then this crisis will end in an overwhelming catastrophe, namely in the 'ecological death' of the earth and its inhabitants. We need first to be clear about the reasons for this crisis of our culture, and then to go on to investigate ways out of it.[1]

The living relationship between a human society and its natural environment is determined by the techniques by which human beings extract what they need to eat and live from nature and return their waste products to it. Since the beginning of industrialization this 'interchange of matter with nature', which is intrinsically as natural as breathing air in and breathing it out again, has been increasingly determined and guided only by human beings, and no longer also by nature. In our 'throwaway society' people think that what they throw away has gone away. But something does not become nothing, so nothing that we throw away has been got rid of. It remains somewhere in nature. Where is that? Who cares?

The natural sciences have invested in human techniques. Technology is the application of natural science, and all the insights of the natural sciences are at one point given technical application and utilized, since 'knowledge is power' (Francis Bacon). Natural science is 'knowing how to control'.

Technologies and natural sciences are always developed out of particular human interests. They are not value free. They are preceded by interests which direct them and make use of them. In turn, these human interests are regulated by the basic values and convictions of a society. These are simply what all those in a society take for granted because they are self-evident and plausible in their system.

Now if a crisis develops in such a life-system which connects a human society with the nature around it, it logically becomes a crisis of the whole system, of attitudes to life, life-style, and not least basic values and convictions. The death of the forests is matched by the spread of psychological neuroses, and pollution of water supplies is matched by the nihilistic feeling about life which many people who live in the great cities have. The crisis which we are experiencing is therefore not just an 'ecological crisis', nor can it be solved by purely technical means. A change in convictions and basic values is as necessary as a change in attitudes in life and life-style.

What interests and what values regulate our scientific technological civilization? To put it simply: the boundless will to rule which has driven modern men and women to seize power over the nature of the earth and continues to drive them on. In what is alleged to be the 'struggle for existence', scientific insights and technical inventions are used by the political will for power, to secure power and to develop power. For us, growth and progress are always measured by an increase in power, in economic, financial and military power. So far a transition from quantitative to qualitative growth has evidently not been achieved.

When we compare our civilizations with pre-modern cultures, the difference is immediately obvious: it is the difference between growth and equilibrium. These pre-modern cultures were by no means primitive or 'underdeveloped', but rather highly complex systems of equilibrium which regulated the relationship of human beings to nature, to one another and to the gods. Only modern Western civilizations are one-sidedly programmed for development, growth, expansion and conquest. Gaining and safeguarding power together with the American 'pursuit of happiness' are the basic values which are in fact operative in our society and regulate everything. Why has this happened?

The deepest reason for this probably lies in the religion of modern humankind. Judaeo-Christian religion has often been made responsible for the human seizure of power over nature

53

and for the boundlessness of the human will to power. Even if normal modern men and women do not consider themselves to be particularly religious, they have still done all they could to fulfil the divine command about their destiny: 'Be fruitful and multiply, fill the earth and subdue it!' They have as it were more than done their duty. This commandment and this view of humankind are more than three thousand years old, but the modern conquest and expansionist culture began in Europe only four hundred years ago. So the reasons must lie elsewhere. In my view they lie in the modern image of God.

Since the Renaissance, in Western Europe God has been understood increasingly one-sidely as 'the almighty'. Omnipotence was regarded as the prime characterisitic of his rule. God is the Lord, the world is his possession, and God can do what he wills with it. He is the absolute subject and the world is the passive object of his rule. In the Western tradition, God kept moving increasingly into the sphere of transcendence, and the world came to be understood in purely immanent and this-worldly terms. God came to be thought of within the world, and as a consequence the world could be thought of without God. It lost its divine mystery as creation and could be scientifically 'disenchanted', as Max Weber aptly described this process. The strict monotheism of modern Western Christianity is an essential basis for the secularization of the world and nature, as Arnold Gehlen already observed clear-sightedly in 1956 in *Urmensch und Spätkultur* (Primal Man and Late Culture): 'At the end of a long history of culture and intellect, the world-view of the *entente secrète*, the metaphysics of powers of life which agree and disagree, has been destroyed. This has come about through monotheism on the one side and scientific technological mechanism on the other, for which in turn monotheism, by ridding nature of demons and gods, has cleared the space. God and the machine have survived the archaic world and now meet each other alone' (285). This is a horrific picture, because not only nature but also human

54

beings have disappeared from this last encounter of 'God' and 'machine'.

As God's image on earth, human beings had to understand themselves as rulers, as the subjects of knowledge and will, facing the world as their passive object to be subdued. For only through their rule over this earth can they correspond to God, the Lord of the world. As God is the Lord and owner of the whole world, so human beings must be concerned to become lords and owners of the earth, in order to prove themselves as the image of their God. Human beings become similar to their God, not through goodness and truth, not through patience and love, but through power and origin. So at the beginning of the modern period Francis Bacon praises the natural sciences of his time: 'Knowledge is power', and through power over nature the image of God in human beings is restored.[2] That this is above all the seizure of power by the male is indicated by our Western forms of speech, which equate 'nature' with 'woman': natural resources are 'exploited', mountains 'forced', rivers 'regulated', the 'virgin forest' is 'penetrated', 'ownerless property' can be taken over, 'secrets' are 'wrenched' from the 'bosom of nature', and so on. This is the language of male violation.

2. The change from one-sided domination to reciprocal community

If we compare this with the famous accusation made by the Indian Chief Seattle in 1855, we shall see where we have got to: 'Every part of this country is sacred to my people, every glittering pine-needle, every sandy beach, all the mists in the dark forests... The rocky hills, the gentle meadows, the bodily warmth of ponies – and of people – they all belong to the same family.'

The change that we must make to experience that we belong 'to the same family' in the nature of the earth, and together with all living creatures, must begin with the image of God on which we orientate ourselves. It is not enough to say with the 1985 German Evangelical Kirchentag: 'The earth is the Lord's.' That is certainly true, and makes it clear that the earth is not our property, and that therefore we are not free to do with it as we like. God has the right to dispose of the earth; human beings have only the right to use it. The earth is more than just a possession of its creator. However, it is not necessary, either, with the 'New Age' movement in India or China to search for the higher wisdom of reverence for all living creatures. We need only return to the original wisdom of our own religious tradition and rediscover what was repressed by that absolutist and masculine modern image of God. This is the rediscovery of the triune God.

This may sound dogmatically orthodox and very old-fashioned, but it contains the future that we seek in order to get out of the modern cul-de-sac in religion and theology. The triune God – as the very name indicates – is not a lonely Lord in heaven incapable of feeling, who subjects all things to himself, but a God who is rich in relationships and capable of relationships, a God in community: 'God is love'. The ancient doctrine of the Trinity was an exposition of the experience that 'God is love'. Father, Son and Holy Spirit live with one another, for one another and in one another in the highest and most supreme communion of love that one can imagine. 'I am in the Father and the Father is in me,' says the Johannine Jesus. The theological tradition has called this trinitarian perichoresis, the mutual interpenetration and reciprocal devotion by which the three divine persons form their unique divine unity.[3] If that is true, then human beings cannot correspond to this triune God through rule and subjection, but only through community and mutuality which furthers life. God's image on earth is not the solitary human subject but true human community. It is not its individual parts, but the community of creation as a whole which reflects God's wisdom and God's beauty.

If we go on to look at nature, we cannot simply say that a God from beyond created this world. More precisely, we must say that God the Father created the world through his Wisdom, the Son/the Daughter (Prov.8), in the Holy Spirit. Therefore everything exists from God and 'in God'. Through his Spirit, God is present in each of his creatures. All life lives from this 'source of life', the divine Spirit. The life-giving Spirit of God is poured out on all creation and forms the community of creation in which all creatures live for one another and with one another and in one another. 'The Spirit is everywhere and present and sustains, nourishes and gives life to all things in heaven and on earth... It is manifest and divine that he pours out his power in all things and through this gives nature, life and movement to all things,' wrote Jean Calvin (*Institutes* I, 13, 14).

'For all existing things are dear to you and you hate nothing that you have made – why else would you have made it? How could anything have continued in existence had it not been your will? How could it have endured unless it had been called into being by you? You spare all things because they are yours, our lord and master who loves all that lives, for our perishable breath is in them all' (Wisdom of Solomon 11.24-12.1).

The perception of the divine Spirit in all things gives rise to a new view of the world: the mechanistic and atomistic picture of the world is replaced by a view of the world in terms of organism and energy. If the Spirit of God is poured out on the whole creation, then the divine spirit creates the unity and the community of all creatures with one another and with God. Life is communication. The life of creation is the communicating community of creation. This fight of the reciprocal relationships of life is brought about by the divine Spirit, which in this respect can also be called the 'cosmic Spirit'. But that means that there are no elements or foundations of the world, or whatever name we may give to 'elementary particles', from which these communicative interconnections could be derived.

According to the 'modern' mechanistic theory, things are

57

primary, and their relations to one another are secondary and determined by natural laws. But according to the new understanding of the world mentioned here, relationships are just as original as things. 'Thing' and 'relationship' are complementary phenomena like wave and particle in an electro-magnetic field. If we understand this field as a field of energy, then the web of relationships has priority over the material concentrations of energy and its reified manifestations. Nothing in reality exists of itself and rests in itself. All beings and entities with life exist and live with one another, for one another and in one another in the wider context of the cosmos. We call the common bond which holds things together 'the cosmic Spirit'. As the divine spirit, this Spirit is one and works to bring unity. It exists of itself and rests in itself and is therefore called God. It is the immanent transcendence in all things. Therefore it is the ground and source of all that does not live of itself but from, with and in others. In this way we describe not only the contingency of reality but also its existence without its own substance, i.e. its existing from God. From the omnipresence of the divine Spirit and through its communion there arise the model and symmetries, the movements and the rhythms, the fields of energy and the material conglomerations: as Werner Heisenberg put it, 'In the beginning was the symmetry. That is certainly more correct than Democritus' theory: "In the beginning was the particle." The elementary particles incorporate the symmetries; they are their simple representations, but they are first a consequence of the symmetries.'[4]

The perception of the divine Spirit in the community of creation corresponds to the new ecological understanding of nature which we seek. The age of the mechanistic worldview was also the age of subjectivity and the sovereignty of humankind over nature. The subjectivity of human beings and the reification of natural beings mutually affected one another. If this division of the common world is not to lead to a mutual destruction of nature and human beings, then we must replace it by a new paradigm of a communicative community of culture and nature based on reciprocity.

This is the original, biblical and Christian insight: by virtue of his creative, life-giving spirit God is in the world and the world is in God: 'The Spirit of the Lord fills the earth' (Wisdom of Solomon 1.7). The variety of creation is the differentiated manifestation of the creative and life-giving Spirit of God.

So 'the earth' is not only the property of 'the Lord' but also the presence of the divine wisdom and the communication of the divine Spirit:

The Holy Spirit is life-giving life,
Mover of the universe and root of all created being,
he purifies the universe from impurity and anoints the wounds,
so he is shining life, worthy of praise,
raising up the universe and reviving it again,

wrote Hildegard of Bingen.[5] An English hymn speaks of the God 'who breathes through all creation'.[6]

> God's Spirit
> sleeps in things,
> dreams in animals,
> awakens in human beings,

says an old saying, thus making it clear that the cosmic Spirit seeks to come to its self-awareness in the human consciousness, and thus consciousness does not separate human beings from nature but connects them with all other creatures. The wisdom of God immanent in the world which gives life to all is as it were the inner side of all things, the side directed towards God. Only those who perceive it find life. Those who fail to do so damage themselves. All those who hate it love death (Proverbs 8.35-36).

What is the significance of this shift in religious attitude, in the relationship with God, for the transformation of the relationship of the world in science and technology?

Modern thought has developed the typically scientific

methods. By them I mean the processes of objectification, analysis, particularization and reduction. What is knowledge? One attempts to isolate an object from its setting in life and then to reduce it to its smallest ingredients, incapable of further division, in order then to reproduce it artificially.[7] To put it more simply, when one can take an object apart and put it together again, then one has come to know it: one has power over it. The old Roman rule about political domination is also practised scientifically on nature: *divide et impera*, divide and rule, rule through dividing. As our language can reveal, we think in terms of the hand which can pick up, hold and possess; we want to 'grasp' everything and when we have 'grasped' it we have the matter 'in our grasp' and control it. We only 'know' something when we can do that. That betrays how much our knowledge of nature is guided by the one, great interest of controlling it.

If by contrast we want to recognize nature as God's creation and perceive the presence of the Spirit of God in nature, then we must abandon this notion of domination and learn another way of thinking: communicative and integrative thinking. We best recognize objects and matters when we leave them in their particular relationships and common features, i.e. do not isolate them, but perceive them in their totality and in their environment. Therefore we have to change our heuristic interest: we no longer want to know in order to dominate but in order to participate, to enter into the reciprocal interest of the living. In antiquity it used to be said that 'knowledge' realizes community. The Hebrew language says that love is 'knowledge'. This mode of total perception and this way of participatory integration of the observer into the observed world is vaguer than the analytical knowledge concerned with domination, but it is richer in relationships. We always know something else only in so far as we love it, and in this love can allow it to be wholly itself. Such total, participatory understanding serves to establish community between human beings and nature. It is capable of leading men and women to reconciliation with nature after the long war against it.

For a long time men and women have regarded nature and themselves only in the interests of their work. They have only seen one side, namely the usable side, of nature, and have overlooked its intrinsic value. There is an old Jewish wisdom of knowing nature as creation and the presence of God. It is the _celebration of the sabbath_, the day of rest, the day of not intervening in nature. According to the first creation story the Creator 'completed' his creation by celebrating the sabbath of the world. God 'rested from all his works'. He blesses his creation through his presence at rest. God no longer acted, but he was wholly there and allowed his creatures to be there. This divine sabbath is the 'crown of creation'; humankind is not. Rather, humankind along with all other creatures is 'crowned' and blessed by the sabbath. In his rest on the sabbath the creator God achieves his goal, and human beings who celebrate the sabbath perceive nature as God's sabbath and allow the world to be God's creation. They heed their own human status and the value of all other creatures.

3. The sabbath of the earth: the divine ecology

Modern Old Testament scholars[8] have been very fond of deriving the modern 'disenchantment', 'de-demonization' and 'secularization of nature', not without some apologetic intent, from the Jewish creation faith which Christianity took over and developed, in order to make the Old Testament understanding of the world topical and relevant for the modern Enlightenment.

The place in which God reveals the mystery of his person is not nature but history, and indeed exclusively human history. From this follows the insight into the 'rooting of creation in the world'. For with the concept of the creation of the world Israel brought about a 'de-divinization of the world' in the 'crisis of the settlement' and the occupation of the land.

The first and second commandments of the Decalogue are 'the key to Israel's understanding of the world'.[9] The battle against idolatry and the mythical transfiguration of the powers of nature, procreation and the capacity to give birth, the fertility of the earth and the cycles of the moon, 'secularized' the world, made it profane.

There is no doubt as to *what* was described in this way, but the words with which it is described are derived from the modern theology of secularization and suggest that the modern view of the world is particularly close to the old Israelite understanding of the world. But it is certainly wrong to assume that. The historical and cultural gap between industrial society and that agricultural world is too great for us to be able to compare modern thought with 'Hebrew thought'. Nevertheless, the apologetic intent is understandable: it was directed against the repaganization of religion by the 'blood and soil' ideology of the Nazis and the 'German Christians'. However, in the apologetic and time-conditioned account of Israelite creation faith and the Old Testament understanding of the world something has been overlooked (or its scope has not been fully grasped), namely the 'sabbath of the earth'. Biblical creation ethics is essentially sabbath ethics, for the sabbath is the law of creation.

According to Exodus 23.10-11, in the seventh year Israel is to leave the land untouched, 'that the poor of your people may eat'. In Leviticus 25.1-7 the law of the sabbatical year is repeated, but another reason is given: 'that the land may celebrate its great sabbath to the Lord'. In Leviticus 25 the sabbatical year legislation is introduced as God's law for the occupation of the promised land and as a guarantee of its possession: 'When you come into the land that I shall give you, the land shall celebrate its sabbath to the Lord... in which you shall not sow your field nor prune your vineyard' (vv.2-24). 'Act according to my ordinances and observe my laws, that you may dwell safely in

62

the land' (v.18). The sabbath rest for the land every seven years contains God's blessing for the land. According to Leviticus 26.1f. this sabbath command takes the place of the fertility gods who guarantee life and blessing for the other peoples: 'You shall not make for yourself any idols… keep my sabbaths and reverence my sanctuary.' Anyone who observes these commandments will enjoy good harvests and live in the peace of the Lord (3-13). But anyone who does not will be visited with terrors, droughts and fevers; his enemies will conquer and rule. 'Then I will make the land desolate… and scatter you among the nations, that your land shall be a desolation, and your cities shall be destroyed. Then the land shall enjoy its sabbaths as long as it lies desolate, while you are in the enemies' land; then the land shall rest and enjoy its sabbaths' (v.34). Verses 42-43 go on to give a remarkable reason for this: 'Then I will remember my covenant with Abraham, and I will remember the land. But the land shall be left by them (sc. Israel), and enjoy its sabbath while it lies desolate without them…' According to II Chronicles 36.19-21, also, the people of Israel is taken into the Babylonian captivity because it did not observe the sabbath year of the earth, 'to fulfil the word of the Lord by the mouth of the prophet Jeremiah, until the land had enjoyed its sabbaths. All the days that it lay desolate it kept sabbath, to fulfil seventy years.'

According to these conceptions of the sabbath year which the land is to celebrate to God the Lord and which is to be respected by the people, this land of God is not given to the people, but rather it seems that the people is given to God's land, in order to care for this land of the Lord. The sabbath year is the mystery of the life of the promised land. If it is observed, the land remains fertile; if it is scorned, the land becomes unfruitful. If it is observed, the people remains in the land. If it is scorned, the Lord has the people deported from the land so that the land can regain its breath and celebrate its sabbaths. Accordingly, God's land seems to be more important than his people. The covenant between God and his land

63

consists in the sabbath year of the earth. For the sake of this covenant Israel comes into the land, and because of the failure to observe the sabbath of the land Israel is deported out of the Lord's land, so that the land is given its due. This is no excessive legalism nor any ancient magic. This is a piece of deep ecological wisdom.

For millennia, most agricultural systems have practised the principle of leaving the land fallow. After a particular sequence of crops a field has to lie fallow for a year in order to recover. The land must be allowed to rest regularly if it is to remain fertile in the long term. The land must regularly be left in peace so that the wild plants and the animals which have been driven away by agriculture can return. Agricultural societies have always been aware that failure to observe fallow periods exhausts the land, causes erosion, decreases the level of the harvests and leads to famine. For agricultural societies the land is the system that supports life. If it is exhausted, then in the end human beings also die or are forced to emigrate. There are many investigations of the connection between land and civilization which show that, for example, the cultures by the Euphrates and Tigris, the Roman cultures in North Africa, the Maya culture in Yucatan and others collapsed because the land was exploited recklessly and short-sightedly and the fertility of the soil was steadily destroyed. Emigration and the 'deportation' of peoples became necessary, to save both the ground and human beings. It was especially the great empires which exploited their granaries and fertile provinces to feed their great cities and armies and also devastated them through pillaging.

Modern industrial society has long changed from being a 'land' economy to being an industrial land economy, with an agri-industry and agribusinesses. The principle of fallow land has disappeared almost completely from industrialized agriculture. Chemical fertilizers give the land what is supposed to be permanent fertility. Monocultures have replaced the old rotation of crops. The 'green revolution' promised bigger and better harvests. Although artificial fertilizers are being used with increasing purpose and intensity, cultivated areas are becoming more and more prone to blight and disease. Crops are declining and costs are increasing. In areas with intensive monocultures over a long period, soil-erosion is extending inexorably, and not just in Third-World countries which are involved in the world market. Herbicides, insecticides and other chemical means produce long-term side effects which seem so destructive that they can no longer be remedied. This damage, which is innocently called 'side effects', is increasingly becoming the main effect. It was and still is short-sighted and suicidal to destroy the basis of one's own life in the long term for the sake of quick profit. It was and still is reckless for the sake of one's own profit to pass on the costs to future generations, who will somehow have to make good the damage and live with it. That is not only morally reckless, but is also the irrational principle of the self-destruction of humankind.

According to the insight of the Old Testament-Israelite belief in God, the wisdom of the sabbath year for the land was evidently the life-sustaining principle of the Creator. Everyone knows that relaxation, rest-time, preserves one's own human strength from exhaustion and restores it. Anyone who observes the weekly sabbath knows the nature of work and love. Can we not understand that what is good for us is also good for the life-giving land, by the fertility of which we all live? According to biblical insight the sabbath year is evidently the ecological wisdom of God, the creator of heaven and earth, who is also called the 'lover of life'. The hopeful and tragic history which Israel experienced in the 'promised land' can be a warning to us who notoriously misuse the sabbath commanments of God. The celebration of the sabbath can become our salvation and the salvation of the earth on which we live. What helps the land and ourselves is not a fine 'fostering and cherishing' nor a grand 'ethic of responsibility' but this simple sabbatical restraint, no longer interfering in creation, this praising 'Let it be'.

65

Why do we not observe the sabbath for ourselves on Sunday and stop the pollution of the environment on Saturday: a day without a car, a day without work? Why do we not take a sabbatical year for ourselves every seven years instead of having early retirement and early pensions? And why do we not encourage the principle of fallow land in agriculture?

According to the Bible, sabbath rules are God's ecological strategy to protect the life which God has made. With its rest and its rhythm of time, the sabbath is also the strategy which wil take us out of ecological crisis and after one-sided progress at the expense of others show us the values of abiding equilibrium and accord with nature.

4. The community of creation as a community under law

(a) Reconciliation with creation

For Christian faith, the spiritual foundations for human return from the heedless exploitation of nature to respectful reconciliation with it lie in the perception of the cosmic Christ and the redemption of the cosmos. This does not do away with personal belief in Christ, nor does it replace it with a religious view of the world, but sees it against the broad horizon of the rule of Christ.[10]

The peace of Christ is personally perceived through faith, in the depth of one's own heart. The inner peace of the soul with God is important because in it that insatiable avarice is overcome by which otherwise the deep anxiety of the heart without God is drowned out. But if this peace of the soul is the peace of Christ, then it points any soul which it affects beyond itself into the communion of all the creatures of the cosmos, since Christ has 'slain enmity' by his death on the cross: enmity of human beings towards themselves and one another, enmity of human beings towards nature, and enmity between the powers of nature itself. The peace of Christ is universal and permeates the whole creation; otherwise Christ is not the Christ of God.

Reconciliation with God is experienced by men and women through faith personally and as a community in Christ. If God himself is present in Christ, then in him human wishes come to rest which are the expression of that longing for God which cannot be assuaged. Men and women can *be* wholly there and need no longer *have* everything. If these wishes find rest, then there is enough for everyone, as was said of the first Christian community in Jerusalem (Acts 4.34). What people experience from God in themselves and among one another as reconciliation leads them beyond themselves and their human world into the breadth of the cosmos: 'All things are reconciled through him on earth or in heaven' (Col.1.20). If the whole creation is not reconciled, then Christ cannot be the Christ of God and the ground of all things. But if it is, then Christians can only encounter other creatures as other people; each creature is a being for whom Christ died in order to take it up into the reconciliation of the world.

Cosmic reconciliation is the restoration of justice in the cosmos. None of these other creatures is destined to be material for human technology and manipulation. In the reconciled community of creation, human beings no longer experience nature as an object or something that confronts them, but as a continuum: they themselves are nature, and nature is in them.

The aggressive ethics of the modern world reflects the mentality of unreconciled human beings and their nihilistic dreams of omnipotence. An ethics of reconciliation serves the common life of all creatures. Over against the aggressive ethics of modernity it must necessarily take on a defensive character, one which preserves life. The Christian confession of creation today is an act of resistance against the destruction of nature and the self-destruction of 'modern man'. But defensive preservation of life and productive furthering of life are not mutually exclusive; they belong together. An ethics of the reconciliation of the needs of human culture with the conditions and powers of regeneration in nature is directed not only towards a just balance but also towards productive co-operation for common survival.

For collaboration on the basis of life together we need a recognition of the particular and common worth of all God's creatures. From the recognition of the worth of creatures on the basis of the love of God for them, the sacrifice of Christ for them and the indwelling of the Spirit of God in them there follows the perception of the rights of any individual creature in the comprehensive law-community of creation. By virtue of reconciliation through Christ the community of creation is the basis for a community of law, not only in the people of God but also in the cosmos. Just as human worth is the source of all human rights, so the worth of creation is the source of the rights of animals, plants and the earth. Human worth is only the human form of the general worth of creation. If there is no codification of the community of creation as a community of law in the creative alliance of God and for its implementation, then all ecological efforts remain poetry and ideology.

Modern ethics, with its aggression towards nature, is a product of the European Renaissance and the European conquests in America, Africa and Asia. It was the Renaissance which first deprived nature of its rights and declared it to be 'property without an owner', which belonged to the one who took possession of it by occupation. It was the conquest which first took possession of the inhabited parts of America, Africa and Asia by force and made them European 'colonies'. Before that, land, water, forest and air were regarded as God's property, left to human beings for common use. Today that is still true of the air that we all must breathe, though the increasing pollution of the air in many cities is already the result of the aggressive and asocial ethics of the modern world. If the community of creation is a community of law, then before all else the rights of the earth as a system and of all kinds of animals and plants must be recognized by human beings and there must be acknowledgment of a codification of the 'rights of the earth' and of animals and plants parallel to the 1948 'Universal Declaration of Human Rights'. There has been such a 'Universal Declaration of Animal Rights' since 1978.[11] An animal is not a thing or a product, but a living being with rights of its own. To respect this fact means putting a stop to the mass keeping of animals for the purpose of 'animal production' and introducing a way of keeping animals which respects their nature. Industrial, hormone-controlled 'animal production' is not only brutality towards animals but is also highly detrimental to human health. The relationship of Christ to the animals is only hinted at discreetly at the end of the temptation story (Mark 1.13): 'And he was among the animals and the angels ministered to him.' This is an allusion to the messianic peace of creation which according to Isa.11 is part of the hope of Israel. Because human beings are physical and natural beings, it is also impossible to realize human rights without at the same time noting the rights of plants and the earth. Without the formulation of their ecological rights and duties, the rights of human beings to life are unrealistic. Rights for non-human creatures can be advocated and implemented if spokesmen and executors are appointed for them in human courts.

(b) Creatures in community under law

Both in Israel in Old Testament times and in the Middle Ages in Europe there were animal trials. But only those animals were punished which attacked, injured or killed human beings; there were not conversely trials of human beings who had committed crimes against animals, except in the case of sodomy. According to Leviticus 20.15, in a case of sodomy the man must die and the animal be throttled. The same thing is said in Article 116 of the Carolina, the 1532 penal law book of Charles V. Trials of pigs were evidently particularly numerous in the Middle Ages, because the pigs were still wild and untamed and occasionally attacked children. There must have been a series of public executions of such pigs, evidently not only before a human audience but also before herds of swine. This curiosity is worth mentioning only because it shows that in the Middle Ages the legal order was evidently not limited to the human community. If the right of human beings against aggressive animals was protected in these trials, then conversely today it is important to protect the rights of animals from aggressive human beings.

Christian faith, like Jewish faith, has particular conceptions of God and law. If God is the creator of heaven and earth, then heaven and earth are his property, and as such must be kept holy and respected. Anyone who calls nature 'God's creation' respects God's law on his earth and resists the human destruction of nature which begins from the fiction that nature is a 'property without an owner' which belongs to the person who first appropriates it.

If God is the owner of his creation, then he has the sole rights of disposal over it. Human beings and animals have only the right to use it in order to nourish themselves and live, within the framework of the general purpose of creation. God wants all his creatures to live together in peace, 'each in his way'. It is not yet quite clear what it means to remove from human beings the right to dispose of those creatures which they can control. But this certainly includes the protection of species, since God created animals and plants 'each after its own fashion' (Gen.1.21,24). The extermination of whole species of plants and animals is consequently to be regarded as sacrilege and punished.

The human ownership of God's creation can only be recognized as just by the use of it in solidarity. This use of it in communal solidarity applies to our present human society. According to the Basic Law of the Federal Republic of Germany, a 'social duty' attaches to property; it may not be used at the cost of other people but only for their benefit. Property also carries an 'obligation to posterity' and may not be used at the expense of coming generations, but only for their benefit. Finally, property carries with it an obligation to the environ-

70

ment; it may only be used 'in association with the environment' and in accord with the natural environment, not at its expense.

Whenever and wherever the reconciliation of the world through God is attested, whether personally, in community or in the cosmos, God's justice is restored and made manifest. The reconciliation on the Great Day of Atonement (Lev.16) of the people of Israel who had become unjust and impure was regarded as being for the justification of Israel and the establishment of God's righteousness, which alone assures life and peace. The reconciliation of the whole cosmos through Christ (Col.1.20) is regarded as the justification of all creatures who have been derived of their rights and violated, and the imposition of the justice of God, which alone ensures life and the peace of creation. The reconciliation of human beings with God, their reconciliation among one another and with themselves, must therefore directly include reconciliation with nature in order to create with it a community under law which is capable of survival.

5. The psychosomatic crisis of modern men and women

'To live in accord with nature' sounds like Rousseau's call 'back to nature', like the Youth Movement and romantic glorification of rural ideals, but it is not. 'To live in accord with nature' means to live one's life in agreement with the laws and rhythms of the earth-system by which we all exist. It also means to exist in harmony with the laws and rhythms of our own bodies. But in order to find this external agreement and this inner harmony, we must relearn the language of nature and hear what it tells us. We must again allow our own body language and may no longer repress it. Evidently we modern inhabitants of industrial society have forgotten both these languages. We no longer pay any attention to them. We drown them out with our own loud business. Therefore nature draws attention to itself all the more noticeably in our own environment by becoming as dumb as the 'silent spring' and slowly dying. Therefore nature

71

announces itself in our own bodies also, through illnesses, and often enough the illnesses are no more than protests against the constant violation of nature by our unnatural and unhealthy way of living. The so-called 'diseases of civilization' are in truth symptoms of a sick civilization.

What motives have made our modern civilizations and ourselves within them contradict our own nature to such a degree?

To the degree to which the modern world, made by human beings in accordance with their own ideas, detached itself from the natural world, the orientation of the human world on the laws of the cosmos and the rhythms of nature was lost. The progress and development of human society no longer correspond with the development of nature, but often enough are carried through against the resistance of nature. Orientation on one's own goals takes the place of concord with nature. This 'scientific-technological civilization', detached from nature, is the great experiment of modern times. It is a colossal human project. If it succeeds, humankind can survive; if it fails, then there will be a tremendous catastrophe which will destroy human beings and other forms of life on this earth. Therefore this 'experiment' has the character of a once-for-all, final 'experiment', and in this sense must be regarded as belonging to the 'end-time'. The 'end-game' of humankind has begun.

With the detachment of this modern project of humanity from the environment of nature, the old notions of the cycles of the regeneration of life and the rhythms of the times, day and night, summer and winter, childhood and old age, were lost. The linear time-line on which everything can be recorded and measured took its place. This is the time-line of goals and purposes which human beings set and pursue. The clock became the omnipresent and almighty timekeeper of the modern world. We all have a watch on our wrist, in our bag, round our neck; there is a clock in the office and in the bedroom, on church towers and factory gates, and it regulates our life from cradle to grave. Whether in working time or leisure, youth or retirement, the clock is always there. It reduces the periods of life that we experience to the data measured in mechanical time. Why? So that we act purposefully as workers, as commuters, as consumers or whatever else we may do. As Lewis Mumford aptly said, the clock became the 'key machine of the modern industrial age'. Any man and particularly any women can feel the consequences of its mechanical rule as forced alienation from the rhythms and cycles of his or her own body. According to mechanical clock-time, every person must be equally available at any time, for the clock does not distinguish between the content of time and takes no account of it.

The alienation of modern men and women from harmony with the nature of their own bodies is also furthered by modern religion and education. Men and women had first laboriously to learn that we also have to become a subject of knowledge and will. They had to learn to control themselves and their bodily urges, to cope with their needs. Self-control and personal control are the supreme principles of industrial society, for only through that control can people be made available at any time. Self-control is also a principle of the modern religion of subjectivity in the moral and pietistic movements.

My father regarded illness as a matter of 'will power', especially in the case of his weakly son. My grandmother taught me the saying:

> To war with oneself
> is the hardest war;
> to conquer oneself
> is the finest victory.

I'm afraid that I was not a very successful victor in this war.

Anyone who goes to Asia or Africa today will see that 'development aid', as we call it, largely consists in subjecting people there to these principles and that our aim to open up those lands to our world market is thwarted by the fact that there people still live according to the other rhythms of nature and the cycles of their own bodies.

73

From its beginnings in Greece, the history of the Western view of humankind has been concerned with the rule of the soul over the body and thus with the instrumentalization and disciplining of the body. The wise soul asserts itself over the foolish body, the commanding ego subjects the obedient body to itself; in consciousness, not in unconsciousness; in the will, not in desire. The soul is always 'above' and the body is always 'below'. The soul rules the body and the body is to obey and serve it; the consciousness determines the unconscious and the ego dominates the body, not vice versa.

The idea of the human centre has undergone a remarkable shift in the history of our civilization: as long as people saw the life of human beings as primarily a matter of breathing air in and out, the centre of life was located in the diaphragm. Life consisted in breathing. The breath is the 'breath of life', and with his or her last breath a person 'expires' (breathes away life). The real symbol for the death of the whole person was the cessation of breathing. Later the life of the human being was seen in his or her great emotions, in the trust of the heart and heartfelt love. There was a recognition of the significance of the circulation of the blood for life. Then the centre of life was located in the human heart. If the heart ceased to beat, a person was regarded as dead. Since about the seventeenth century, the view has established itself that the human brain is the centre of human life. Being human is understood as being the subject of understanding and will. This subjectivity was located in the brain, behind the eyes; since then 'brain death' has become the real symbol for the death of the human person. (Japanese doctors report that they still have difficulties with this Western anthropology, because according to Japanese culture person and nature form a continuum and cannot be contrasted.) The other parts of the body, even the heart, are consequently made into interchangeable parts of that machine which the human subject possesses and dominates. No wonder that the modern inhabitants of industrial society have essentially the same relationship to their bodies as they do to their cars.

Certainly one can celebrate this image of human nature as the foundation of the great European history of freedom, but it also has its price in the no less great history of European oppression. People who no longer perceive their own bodies nor understand the language of their bodies nor heed their demands become cramped and impoverished. Their relationship to their own bodies exactly corresponds to their relationship to the nature around them, and vice versa. The destruction of the outside environment corresponds to our illnesses within, what we call the diseases of civilization. To put things simply, each of us also carries around the ecological crisis in our own bodies.

Here we must ask back a theological question. Modern theology has allowed itself to enter into the development of this civilization and has served the religion of the modern age. It has taken over the separation of human history and non-human nature, and spoken of God's revelation and presence only in human nature, not also in non-human nature. At a very early stage it took up the separation of soul and body and found God's spirit only in the soul and not in the human body. It taught that human beings were to be the image of God only in the soul, and not in their bodies.

These divisions then gave rise to a godless view of nature and a natureless view of God; a divine appreciation of the soul and a god-less repression of the body. All the religious taboos were taken away from nature, so that it was defenceless and delivered over to the human will to power. But does not God, the creator of heaven and earth, also speak his own language to other creatures through the laws of the earth and the characteristics of other creatures? Does not the God who has created human beings as wholes, with souls and bodies, also speak to the human consciousness and the soul through body language?

Amazingly enough, it was Christian mysticism which taught

us to note the language of God in nature. Hildegard of Bingen and Francis of Assisi are universally-known representatives of a cosmic mysticism in Christianity. But we also find this in the modern mystic Ernesto Cardenal, the poet and revolutionary from Nicaragua. In his book *To Live is to Love*, he writes:

All animals who lift their voices at dawn sing to God. The volcanos and the clouds and the trees cry to us about God. The whole creation cries to us penetratingly, with a great cry, about the existence and the beauty and the love of God. The music roars it into our ears and the landscape calls it into our eyes... In all of nature we find God's initials and all God's creatures are God's love letters to us. All of nature burns with love created through love, to light love in us... Nature is like a shadow of God, a reflection of his beauty. The still, blue lake is a reflection of God. In every atom lives an image of the Trinity, a figure of the trinitarian God. And also my own body is created to love God. Each of my cells is a hymn about the creator and an ongoing declaration of love.[12]

So that no one will think that this is typically Catholic praise of 'natural theology', let me also quote the Reformer John Calvin, who perceived the presence of God in nature in just the same way. In his *Institutes of the Christian Religion* he wrote:

The highest goal of the blessed life is the knowledge of God. The access to blessedness should not remain closed to anyone; for this reason God has not only given to the human what we call the seed of religion. He revealed himself and is still revealing himself today in the whole structure of the world in such a way that human beings cannot open their eyes without necessarily seeing him. His essence is indeed incomprehensible, so that his divinity is inaccessible to all human understanding. But he has imprinted on his individual works reliable marks of his glory, and they are so clear and impressive that even for the most foolish, every excuse claiming not to know is made impossible... Wherever the eye goes, there is all around no minor part of the world in which there is not at least some little spark of his glory to be seen. But all the burning torches in the house of the world, which are set for the glorification of the creator, are spreading their light for us in vain. From all sides they shine their light over us, but we are lacking the eyes, we are blind.[13]

And is it not in fact the case that an unprejudiced look at nature and at natural history could convince us of the existence, the wisdom and the beauty of God? God himself must reveal himself to us, so that we recognize him and know who he is. According to the testimony of the Bible this self-revelation of God takes place in the history of the liberation of Israel from servitude in Egypt, as the Torah says from the First Commandment on, and in the story of Christ, his sacrifice in death for us and his resurrection from the dead before us, as the gospel says. This is rightly called the self-revelation and the self-communication of God to us.

But the knowledge of God does not stop with this; that is where it begins. Those who recognize and believe in God in the history of Israel or in the history of Christ as their God and Lord recognize his activity everywhere. Those who have experienced God as love in faith will find the demonstrations of this divine love in all created beings. Those who know the name of God will discover the wisdom and the beauty of God in all his works. The knowledge of God in nature is no saving way to God. True 'natural theology' is simply a recognition of the God who has revealed himself and whom one trusts. Therefore 'natural theology' does not make anyone blessed, but it can make people wise in their dealings with nature because they learn to note the language of God in nature. We need a new, Christian 'natural theology', not so much for the sake of God as in earlier times as for the sake of nature and its worth.

Those who know God because they believe in his revelation

see the 'traces of God' in nature. For them nature becomes the parable of the coming kingdom of God. They perceive any creature, even the smallest and most fragile, the 'lilies of the field and the birds of the air', as a living promise of the coming glory of God. The whole created world of heaven and earth is then one great real promise of the coming world of God. Present earthly reality becomes transparent to the future divine glory which is to be made manifest in it. Therefore creation as a whole and each individual creature in it is an 'open system', open for its true future in the presence of God. It is probably time that Protestant theology rediscovered the breadth of creation and its future with the help of such a 'natural theology'. We will live 'in accord with nature' when we discover God in nature and learn to respect nature in God.

If we find the 'traces of God' in the nature of our environment, then we can discover the 'image of God' in ourselves. This is a mirror which is certainly even clearer, in which God manifests himself and we can recognize him when we know God and are aware of who God is. Christian theology has unfortunately for a long time hindered this insight by teaching that the image of God is mirrored only in the human soul and not in the human body. It taught that only the soul which dominates the body bears the seal of the image of God. However, this contradicts the biblical understanding according to which God created human beings in his image, 'male and female he created them' (Gen.1.27). 'Male and female' means the whole human constitution, body and soul. It is not the sexless soul which elevates itself above the male or female body, but the whole form of a human being which is the image of God. Therefore women and men are directed towards one another, and only together are they the whole image of God on earth. Human community is to be like God, and it is to be made like God by women and men, parents and children. In the real personal and social form of human beings, soul and body, conscious and unconscious, voluntary and involuntary, interpenetrate and influence one another. The body constantly talks to the soul.[14] Our unconscious movements and needs constantly influence our consciousness. The body has its own language. It has its own memories, which are often different from the deliberate memories of the soul. Therefore it also has its own reactions, which often diverge from those which human beings want to express, and betray something other than what they say. We will again be able to 'live in accord with nature' if we transcend the individual and social repressions of our body by the consciousness and will of the soul and come into a living harmony with ourselves and one another. However, the rediscovery and regaining of such harmony with ourselves and one another can become a rebellion against the disciplinary measures of modern civilization which make us sick. So we will seek this harmony of body and soul in ourselves all the more strongly, the more we perceive the divine worth of the body and thus recognize God's spirit *in* our body and our body *in* the Spirit of God, as Paul puts it in his language; 'The body belongs to the Lord and the Lord to the body... praise God in your spirit' (I Cor.5.13,20).

Finally, it is helpful to see modern scientific and technological civilization, this colossal human project, not simply from inside but also from outside. Seen from inside, modern civilization rises up over nature and dominates it with a thousand arms, holding it firm in its 'grasp' with ten thousand hands. With motorways and railroads, great cities and industrial areas, human civilization girdles the earth like a web. Human beings seem to be on top and the earth underneath. But it looks quite different from outside. The pictures which rockets and satellites have taken of the earth show that humankind lives in, not on, this earth. With its atmosphere and its biosphere, the constant incursion of solar energy, the regular revolutions of the earth, stable temperatures and regular shifts of temperatures, the earth is like one living organism, an open system which breathes in energy and regulates itself. That is the so-called Gaia hypothesis that Lovelock and Margulis have developed. Human beings entered into the evolution of this living organism 'earth' at a relatively late stage. They develop their cultures in the comprehensive organism earth, but they do not control it. Rather, humankind is dependent on the functioning of the comprehensive organism earth for its extension and further development, and must harmonize and reconcile this extension and development with the environmental conditions. If one looks at humankind from the outside in this way, then the question arises whether it is a colossal cancerous growth in the comprehensive organism earth or whether human civilization will one day develop into something like its nerve system. 'Living in accord' with nature means bringing the further development of human civilization into tune with the conditions of the comprehensive earth organism and reconciling it to that. Humankind has not yet discovered the role intended for it in this overall organism. It would help us if we again recognized the wisdom of God in the laws and conditions of the system earth and in our own psychosomatic constitution. Living in accordance with God means living truly human lives, but we can live in accordance with God only if we also live in accordance with nature, in and with which we are made and through which God speaks with us.

6. The sabbath of humankind: the divine therapy

Sunday is being very much talked about. Modern high-tech industries call for the introduction of Sunday working in order to be able to use their expensive machines better by flexible working hours. Their arguments are clear: there is increasing competition especially from the Far East; jobs are in danger; the complicated processes of production cannot be stopped on Friday and started up again on Monday. Even though in the Federal Republic of Germany Sunday is protected by the constitution, from an economic perspective it seems irrational and expensive. Why not deal with it in a different way, if that seems useful?

This public discussion is occasion enough for Christians to

ask themselves what they are really doing on Sunday and what their day of rest is worth. Regarding it just as an interruption of everyday work causes great difficulties for many people: they do not know what to do with the free day. Therefore in some families the arguments are more frequent on Sunday. Most murders in families take place on Sunday evening. It is not without danger to have a day of celebration when you don't know what you should celebrate. It is difficult to introduce a day of rest when you don't know how you should rest.

Our day of celebration goes back to the sabbath commandment of Israel. Our Sunday derives from the legislation of the emperor Constantine in 312. Since then, the 'Day of the Sun' has been meant to be kept free from work. It was at the same time that day after the Jewish sabbath which the Christians had celebrated from the beginning as the day of Christ's resurrection. The universal commandment 'You shall hallow the day of celebration' only blurs the internal differences. It is therefore sensible and helpful to look back at the Jewish sabbath through the Christian Sunday and rediscover its wisdom.

Six days you shall labour, and do all your work; but the seventh day is a sabbath to the Lord your God; in it you shall not do any work, you, or your son, or your daughter, your manservant, or you maidservant, or your cattle, or the sojourner who is within your gates; for in six days the Lord made heaven and earth, the sea, and all that is in them, and rested the seventh day; therefore the Lord blesed the seventh day and hallowed it.

This commandment is the longest and therefore, as the rabbis say, the most important. It is also the finest commandment, because it is a commandment for a life that is a healthy and happy life. It is the feast of creation on which the beauties of existence are to be celebrated. It is unique, in that all the other religious festivals and fast days in the church's year are festivals and feast days of salvation history. The salvation and blessing of creation do not appear in them.

First let us look at the commandment, then at the reason given for it, and then try to understand the two together.

The commandment says: you shall work six days, and on the seventh day you shall do no work. Nor shall your son nor your daughter nor your manservant nor your maidservant nor your cattle nor the stranger who is within your gates. The command to work is addressed to the one to whom it is spoken, but the commandment to rest applies to all equally. On the sabbath all are blessed equally and with equal rights: men and women, parents and children, overseers and workers, natives and foreigners, human beings and animals. They are all to enjoy their rest equally and together. All differences which have come into being as a result of sharing and organizing work are done away with again on the seventh day of each week. No one can celebrate this sabbath at the expense of others. The sabbath is celebrated together or not at all. In that celebration of the sabbath the community of creation between human beings and animals is restored. If according to the creation story a command to 'rule over' the animals is associated with the definition of human beings as being in the image of God, then according to the fourth commandment this is rightly caried out and consummated on the sabbath day.

It is also striking that work and rest are related to nature. At that time 'work' was direct, physical work within nature, to secure food, protection, a home, clothing and energy. 'Rest' on the sabbath does not mean 'Have a rest and refresh yourself', but, 'You shall do no work'. On this day you shall not intervene in nature, but leave the fields, meadows, trees and animals to rest so that they can take breath. The day of rest is not primarily there for human beings but for the nature within which human beings work. It has not only therapeutic significance, but also ecological significance for the nature within which this work is done. On the sabbath day nature is not a field of work for men and women but God's creation, which they are to allow to rest and thus to be what it is in order to enjoy along with it the blessing which the creator has bestowed on all his creatures.

The day of rest is the day for not interfering in nature, whether in external nature or in the nature of one's own body. It is thus the feast of creation on which one rediscovers the beauty of created things and perceives the value of all the things which one has seen during work only in terms of utility. In the relationship between human beings, common interest and projects fade into the background and people discover interest in one another and take one another seriously as persons. The sabbath night was often celebrated as a night of love.

When the tumult of one's own work dies down, when reflections and projections of thought come to rest and people learn to become still, they perceive something that otherwise they may miss: hearing the silent presence of God and his nearness in the stillness around. 'God is present, all is silent for us...', rightly runs the Sunday hymn of the Protestant mystic Gerhard Tersteegen. One is reminded of the prophet Elijah's experience of God on Horeb: in despair at the ineffectiveness of his message and the godlessness of his people, Elijah goes to Horeb, the mountain of God, to seek God. He stands on the mountain and experiences a storm, 'but the Lord was not in the storm'. Then he experiences an 'earthquake', 'but the Lord was not in the earthquake'. Then he sees a fire around him, 'but the Lord was not in the fire'. Finally he hears a 'still small voice'; he covers his head, for the Lord is there. There is also something of this experience of God in what Karl Rahner called 'silent mystery', in the experience of the sabbath. The sabbath is a day for meditation.

The weekly rhythm of work and rest is grounded in the rhythm of the creator and his whole creation. Did God make the world in six or seven days? The problem does not lie in the numbers. They are meant symbolically and not literally. The problem is whether the creation is a 'six-day work', as the Christian tradition has often called it, and what its creator really added to it on the seventh day. God 'completes' his creation on the seventh day: by what? What does he add? The answer is quite amazing. The work of creation has really come to an end with the sixth day: after the creation of human beings we read, 'And God saw all that he had made, and behold it was very good' (Gen.1.31). The creator as it were detaches himself from his creation. He retreats and stands back, so that he can see it, and then pronounces a verdict. All creation and all activity is a matter of coming out of oneself and giving oneself. Every artist puts his soul into his work of art. Therefore he or she has only finished with the work of art when it is possible to stand back and return to oneself, to retreat and be pleased with the work. Only then can one leave a work of art as it has become, without correcting it or improving it further. After action comes letting things be, and after creation comes existence. Is this second element also to be called 'creative'? When children grow up, parents know that they themselves have to draw back so that their children can become free and achieve themselves. Retreating is certainly painful, but for a child it is highly creative, beause as a result the child is given space for self-development. It is just the same when the creator has completed creating, stands back from his creation and lets it be what it has become, and finds pleasure in it.

But what does God add on the seventh day of his work of creation which he already found very good on the evening of the sixth day? He 'completed' his work by resting from it, and 'blessed and hallowed' this seventh day (Gen.2.2,3; Ex.2.11). He rests from his work and does not intervene in it further. In rest he experiences and feels as it were all the creatures he has made. He also rests in his works. These exist before him, and he exists before them. They are mutually present. That is expresed by the prophets with the image of heaven and earth becoming the 'dwelling place' of God, in which God takes his rest (Isa.66.1; Acts 7.49). If God has created this world to dwell and rest in it, then the sabbath day with the rest of God is in fact the goal of the whole work of creation. God creates in order to arrive at this rest; he does not rest in order to create again.

By his rest the creator *blesses* this seventh day. Elsewhere powers and works are blessed, but here it is a day. Elsewhere God blesses through grace; here he blesses by being at rest. If a day is blessed, then a rhythm comes into being in time which benefits all creatures who live in time. So it is there for everyone to the same degree. If God blesses by resting and not intervening, then he lets all things be what they are. He gives no greater blessing than this imageless omnipresence of God, which breaks down all barriers and is won back from all activity.

By his presence at rest the Creator *hallows* the seventh day. Before the people and the land of Israel are declared 'holy', the sabbath is hallowed. After the second destruction of the temple the sabbath day became as it were Israel's cathedral, and Judaism became a 'religion of time' (Abraham Heschel). Neither spaces, nor hills, nor cities received God's first holiness, but the sabbath in the rhythm of time. How is this day hallowed? Not through religious or moral efforts but through the relaxation and giving up all work to that point at which people experience that they *are*, that they are simply there and perceive things and people in their creaturely worth and beauty. Purposeful activity disappears and utilitarian values no longer have a place. 'Time is money' no longer appplies. Just being, without planning or being useful, is splendid. The sabbath is this eternity in time.

If we sum up the commandment and the reason for it, we get the following picture: God creates and shapes a rich and colourful world in order to celebrate the feast of creation with all his creatures on the sabbath. Therefore the sabbath is the consummation of creation; without it creation is incomplete and remains insignificant.

Men and women can be in harmony with God the creator of the world through their work. Strictly speaking, the point of comparison with human work is God's 'doing', i.e. forming and shaping, not the divine 'creating', i.e. actually calling into being. But even more, men and women correspond to the creator God by resting on the seventh day, for on it and through

85

it they accord with the God who completes, rests, celebrates. The feast day is not there to restore one's strength so as to be fit again for Monday. On the contrary, all six working days serve the feast of creation.

What is the significance of this life in harmony with God in work and rest? It expresses the worth of men and women, the fact that they are in the image of God. Therefore the 'right to work' is irrevocably part of human worth. Unemployment damages God's image in humankind. But the 'right to rest' on the festival day of creation is also part of human worth. The 'brute being without peace and quiet', Goethe's Faust and the modern workaholic, who are always afraid of getting a raw deal and can never work enough, who always have to work and never rest, are caricatures of God, not his image. In the divine creation-rhythm of work and rest, working and celebrating, human life corresponds to the creator, remains healthy and allows the other creatures to live in peace.

What do we do on Sunday? What is our festival worth? The question was badly put. We would do better to ask: what do we allow to happen on Sunday? What do we let be? To open up the conversation, let me make some personal suggestions.

We reckon the day from morning to evening. The creation story speaks of 'evening and morning'. It helps me to begin the day of celebration on Saturday at noon and end it on Sunday afternoon. In that case one relaxes on Saturday, and at least on this evening one can trace something of Israel's sabbath rest. It is possible to observe Saturday as a rest day for nature and spend at least this day without exhaust fumes and lawnmowers and so on. In weekend prayer one can receive that grace which says 'All's well that ends well', because it makes good what we have done badly or neglected. On this afternoon and evening we can relax again with toning-up exercises, so that we can again feel the bodies that we are. Instrumental reason is then out of a job and the perceptive reason again perceives the ground of all things. On Sunday morning we are then ready to celebrate the day of Christ's resurrection, and on it the first day of the new creation of all things, and to perceive that future in which all things will be completed, because God finally comes to come to rest in his world. Then it can be said that 'All's well that begins well'.

Are Saturday and Sunday available for flexible working hours? I do not think so, since they are not part of the world of work, but part of the worth and self-esteem of human beings, men and women, parents and children, natives and foreigners, human beings and animals. We would be giving up ourselves if we gave up the sabbath and Sunday. We are made in the image of God and not to be the slaves of work and consumerism. We are children of God and subject to no one. Sabbath and Sunday belong to God, so that we human beings can become a blessing to one another and to creation.

7. China between Tao and Mao

Nowhere else in the world can the change from the pre-modern world to the modern age be observed so strikingly as in China. The whole country is a giant building site: from the hut to the high-rise building, from the mule track to the expressway, from the village to the mass industrial conurbation, from agricultural communities to a centralized industrial society. Today the Chinese people are organizing themselves to set out from the culture of harmony with nature to the culture of progress in world history. We can see these two basic models of human culture clearly. We can understand the reasons for abolishing the old Asian system. We can understand the reasons for adopting the early-European belief in progress in the form of Marxist-Leninist Socialism. But we can also see the terrible contradictions between the modern culture of progress and the nature which supports it, and ask whether and how the wisdom of ancient Chinese culture can be used to heal the wounds of the modern world. And because the basic problem of our modern world is brought out in the contradictions between the old culture of equilibrium and the modern belief

87

in history, I shall now reflect on a journey through China and develop more general considerations from my reflections. I think that the older history-of-religions discussion as to whether the religious sense of the Chinese is immanent or transcendent and whether today's Maoism is to be interpreted in religious or secular terms is outdated. I shall begin from the paradigms of 'equilibrium' and 'progress' because they are more capable of grasping the unities of culture, ideology and religion.

(a) Harmony in the scheme of 'nature'

When you enter the old imperial palace in Beijing, the so-called 'forbidden city', through the 'Gate of Eternal Peace', you are faced with the centre of the 'middle kingdom', the middle of the world. The layout reflects perfect harmony; everything matches: left and right, height and width, walls and roofs, foreground and background.

Here there is no history of style nor any break in style, but only the one, timeless, uniform harmony. Before you stands the 'Hall of Supreme Harmony', behind that is the 'Hall of Central Harmony' and after that the 'Hall of Heavenly Harmony'. In the central temple of the Chinese world the longing for 'harmony' dominates even the old 'political religion' of the Middle Kingdom. This temple area is in the south of Beijing. Architecturally, here the circle and the number three dominate the scene: the heavenly temple has three storeys and three round roofs on the square of the earth. The heavenly altar of heaven has three times three (i.e. nine) tiers, each with nine tiles in a circle, etc. The circle is the symbol of heaven; the right angle the symbol of the earth.

The basic notion of 'harmony' also dominates the old Chinese religion of the *I Ching*. The Chinese people accepted alien religions on the basis of this fundamental pattern. To make a very rough classification, it might be said that ancient Chinese Taoism is the religion of natural harmony; Confucianism is the religion of social harmony; and Buddhism, whether

Amitabha or Zen, is the religion of inner spiritual harmony. However, this is not a prestabilized, fixed harmony, as Leibniz assumed, but a flowing harmony which embraces pulsating life, the rhythms of nature and the cycles of history, and through which human beings attempt to attune themselves to life, nature and history and influence them. The differences in history and the contradictions of life are embraced within the fluid equilibrium of Yin and Yang. Natural processes are not analysed as atoms and relations but understood as totalities through five fundamental organic processes. The incomprehensible 'one' develops in the many, and the many finds a way to harmony in the one: 'The way begets one; one begets two; two begets three; three begets the myriad creatures. The myriad creatures carry on their backs the yin and embrace in their arms the yang and are the blending of the generative forces of the two' (*Tao te Ching*, 42).[15]

The economic reality which underlies this ideal of equilibrium which dominates religion and culture is 'the rice field' (E.Wickert). A people which feeds on rice is dependent on the culture of the rice field. Rice needs water and sun. The fields require communal manual labour and intensive cultivation. Just as the fields depend on one another for their irrigation, so the workers and owners depend on one another. No one may 'dig the water away' from another. The rice field resists both the capitalist principle of competition and individualism. It calls for communalism and requires comradely work. Planting and harvest must be adjusted to the times, the season and phases of the moon. The feasts of human religion are at the same time the feasts of nature, which regenerates itself and gives life. The terraces of the rice field are works of art, thousands of years old. They are the product of countless generations, which have worked on them and lived on them. Therefore the dead are buried on the margins of the rice fields. They are constantly present to the living. Each generation feels itself bound to its ancestors in the rice field like the links in a long chain. But the ancient Chinese ancestor cult is not superstition, as the Pope claimed in the seventeenth century and Protestant missionaries claimed in the nineteenth century; it is the natural worship of those who used to work in the rice fields and whose work made possible the life of the living. And because ancestor worship obliges one to hand on the rice field to one's children, ancestor worship is simply a good spiritual expression of the contract between the generations.

The political religion of ancient China was celebrated in the imperial cult until the year 1911. No matter what other religious influences were accepted by the Chinese court, Confucianism was always able to assert its predominance. The religious legitimation which it provided for rule was only replaced by Marxist-Leninist-Maoist socialism. According to Confucian teaching the world of human beings and the world of heaven, understood as the deity (*tian*), are linked. If all living beings follow the way of heaven (*tiantao*), then peace, prosperity and harmony prevail. The human being stands between heaven and earth as the corner of the cosmic order and as the mediator of the rhythms and cycles of the universe. This human being is represented by the 'son of heaven', who has to fulfil the task of heaven in the human world and in the natural world. The 'way of the ruler' (*wang-tao*) is in accord with the 'way of heaven' (*tiantao*) and radiates the effects of his power over all. He puts humanity and the nature of the earth on the right course. If the emperor fails in this heavenly task, then his rule loses its legitimation and the task passes on to someone more worthy. Because it is the charge from heaven itself which legitimates the ruler who is revered as son of heaven, his claim to rule extends over the whole earth and all the peoples under the earth. It is therefore in essence universal. On the other hand, however, his rule must correspond to the rule of heaven. Heaven has an effect on earth like Yin and Yang, i.e. not through violence but through the fluid equilibrium, less through intervention than through the weight of its own being. Accordingly the Son of heaven also rules through his radiance and his attraction as an abiding pole in the centre of the world, not through active intervention. He rules through effective non-intervention (*wuwei*). He goes to no one, but all come to him, since through his central being and through the rites of heaven which he performs in the heavenly temple he mediates the harmony of human beings and earth with the way of heaven. Although in political practice a legally regulated system of reward and punishment ensured the observance of social norms in ancient China, 'non-violent rule' through the existence of the middle point and enduring mediation with heaven remained the ideal of the Chinese emperor.

The emperor of China was probably the last *priest-emperor* in the world. Whereas in the Roman empire the imperial priestly title 'Pontifex Maximus' was already transferred to the Pope by Gelasius I and the subsequent difference between Pope and Emperor began to secularize European politics, in China the unity of religion and politics remained until 1911. In Confucian teaching there is no difference between sacred and profane. The emperor stood at the head of a patriarchal hierarchy which gave orders to the whole empire. Just as he derived his office from his status as *paterfamilias*, so each official in the kingdom and each father of a family derived his authority from that of the emperor. In his person the supreme power of the ruler was united with the supreme priestly worth and this had to find recognition 'under heaven', i.e. all over the earth and among all peoples. In the spring, to the sound of flutes the Emperor as the 'first man of the land' drew the first furrows in the field alongside the agricultural altar in Beijing. At the altar of the gods of the soil and the fruits of the field he prayed to heaven for the seed to prosper and gave thanks for the harvests, for only the blessing of nature guaranteed peace in the kingdom. The head of the Commission of Rites was one of the most senior officials in the kingdom. The so-called emperor cult is grounded in this cultic significance of the emperor. The representative of heaven, responsible for the whole universe, was at the head of political religion. Just as he showed honour to heaven in the *kow-tow*, so too due honour was shown to him. His priestly rule called for the virtue of devotion not only to himself but also to his imperial ancestors and above all to the high ruler of heaven, whom he and they served and by whom they were legitimated. Court ceremonial and the priestly rites of the emperor show the harmony of the human world which was striven for in the unity of the universe. The Chinese imperial idea embraced the harmony of culture and nature: the human ruler is responsible for peace not only in the world of men but also in the world of nature. In this respect one can speak of an idea of rule which is archaic but nevertheless ecological. Political religion was founded in the harmony of heaven and earth. It was a natural political religion.

(b) Progress in the scheme of 'history'

Our Chinese interpreter and guide was called Ku. He was an educated, intelligent student from Beijing. Nevertheless he did not know the *Tao te Ching*; he had only heard of Confucius in school but not read him; and he borrowed the *Discourses of the Buddha* from me and read it on an overnight train journey from Guilin to Wuhan. His language and ideology were moulded by the views that 'China was backward', the revolution brought the 'great leap forward', China needs 'progress' and cannot stand still in history and Deng Xiao Ping's policy is serving to 'modernize' China on the Western model with the help of Western technology.

The bourgeois ideas of the Western world were brought to China by Sun Yat-Sen and its socialist ideas by Mao Tse Tung; there they have been 'Sinified'. It is remarkable that the ideology of the underdeveloped and early industrialized lands, i.e. of Socialism, rather than the ideology of the highly industrialized nations has found a home in China. Since the Opium Wars Western capitalism has had a destructive and deterrent effect on China. Russian Socialism, Marxism-Leninism, had come into being from a similar situation in Russia and therefore seemed to the Chinese people to be liberating and to promise a future. The names of Marx, Lenin and Mao indicate the movement and the change in this ideology. Its origins lie in the combination of an idealistic German philosophy of history with the misery of the alienated industrial proletariat of Europe. The content of this ideology is the modern scheme of history with its ideas of 'progress' and linear, purpose-orientated 'time'.

The vehicle of this ideology is the alienated industrial proletariat of the mass conurbations. The certainty of this ideology lies in the inevitability of the history with which the proletariat will liberate itself and in the role of the Party, which will lead the proletariat to accomplish its role in history. The aim is for humankind, united and under a centralized rule, to become the subject of its own history. To compare this scheme of the modern world with the ancient Chinese scheme, I shall stress some of its most important characteristics as they appear to a self-critical Western eye.

The modern view of the world as 'history' evidently came into being in modern times in the wake of the industrial revolutions of Europe and America. To the degree to which a human world, planned and made by human beings, detached itself from the world of nature, the orientation of the human world on the rhythms of nature and the laws of the cosmos was lost. The development of human history no longer corresponded to the development of nature, since the development of human history consisted in the subjugation of nature and the exploitation of its resources, rather than in harmonious accord with it. Nature was replaced by orientation on self-appointed human goals. The more people experience themselves as subjects of history and make nature the object of their knowledge and work, the more they must ask what future can give meaning to their historical experience and purpose to their historical praxis. If their plan for the future is clear, then the aims and goals for individual steps in the history of its realization can be defined. And these steps are then called 'progress'. Progress is therefore always simply meant to be a step towards a better future. With the detachment of the human

93

world from the natural environment, the cyclical conception of time which was read off the rhythms of nature is replaced by the linear concept of time. Remarkably, however, the early industrial idea of progress is embedded in a twofold scheme of history which corresponds to the old harmonious relationship between culture and nature: there is the progressive history of the world spirit and there is the human history of progress. Human subjective history must correspond to the objective laws and tendencies of history if it is not to degenerate into inhuman arbitrariness. This ideological duplication achieves the legitimation of disputed subjective human history by unassailable objective historical regularities: the various human histories on this earth and the various sequences of progress are elevated to become 'history'. 'History' takes the place of Tientao, the will of heaven – or in European terms, divine providence. The Chinese expression for 'revolution' is 'ko-ming', and means the acceptance of a charge given by heaven (Julia Ching). Only if one believes in 'history' can one speak of the objective need for progress and the inevitability of the intended development, classify cultural forces as 'backward' and 'progressive', and say that 'history' supports those who have the right social praxis by rewarding them with success. This of course ends up as a tautology, since the successful are proved right by history. Through Marx, the idealistic philosophy of history and historical pragmatism are fused into a single modern ideology.

The economic reality underlying this conception of history which dominates religion and culture is not the rice field but the industrial concern. Both those who profit as workers for industrial production and those who profit as owners of capital for industrial production are dependent on industrial culture. Production is directed towards the maximizing of productivity and profit. More must be produced and more consumed. Production is therefore programmed for growth and expansion, for innovation and the accumulation of power. Because it is in principle infinite, it is also universal in its tendency. One of its most important stimuli is 'free competition' or 'the fight of all against all'. Industrialization therefore leads inexorably to a competitive and individualistic society. The fight for market-share and jobs dominates the scene. As workers, everyone is for him- or herself. The family no longer has a role. The natural adult community of generations is replaced by the free association of individuals. What has happened in the highly industrialized West after two hundred years has to be introduced by state pressure in the great industrial conurbations of China: birth control. The modern Chinese one-child marriage is enforced by tax legislation. It is necessary in the great conurbations and can be implemented there, but not on the land. Therefore legislation has been relaxed for the agricultural population. The one-child family and the cremation of the dead without distinction is presumably breaking up the old Chinese family culture, just as the family has been broken up in the West as the primary institution for social aid and the place where people are at home. It would be good if the Chinese people and its government could recognize the human cost of Western 'modernization' which consists in individualization, isolation and human alienation. Does the street committee replace the village community? Does the Party replace the family? Can state social welfare replace family solidarity? Certainly modern industrial society must pay through industrial concerns, local government organizations and the state for what it has destroyed. But are the gains really higher than the costs?

The religious roots of Western industrial culture and its ideologies, whether capitalist or socialist, have rightly been seen in so-called Abrahamic religion – in Judaism, Christianity and Islam. These three religions are religions of hope and therefore religions of historical existence. Nature plays a comparatively small role in them. The father of their faith is Abraham, to whom 'the Lord' says: 'Go from your country and your kindred and your father's house to the land that I will show you. And I will make of you a great nation, and I will bless you, and make your name great, so that you will be a blessing' (Gen.12.1-2). For the three Abrahamic religions this exodus of Abraham from his home, family and friends and his 'long march' through strange lands in search of a future home is the model for the hope of a coming kingdom of God. And because it is said that in Abraham 'all the generations on earth shall be blessed' (Gen.12.3), these Abrahamic religions are world religions and in principle have a universal concern. They must permeate the whole world in mission, in order to prepare all peoples for this future kingdom of God. They are not religions of human equilibrium with the natural environment in the sequence of generations and the greater community of the state. They are religions of human alienation from the past and present for the sake of God's greater future. In other words, they are not nature religions but religions of history; not religions of equilibrium and harmony but religions of conflict and hope. They are – as Asian people put it – 'aggressive religions'. But they have become the religious basis for the development of modern industrial ideologies which outline the scheme of 'history' and are programmed for 'progress' and 'expansion'.

A clear sign of this is the parallel in the change of festivals and feast days. When Israel came into the land of Canaan, it took over the agricultural festivals of seedtime and harvest, winter and summer solstices, and gave them new content as commemorations of its own salvation history. Israel 'historicized' the nature festivals. Socialist industrial society did something similar: the historical festivals of revolution and 'Labour Day' took the place of the old religious festivals. How does 'history' legitimate political rule? If the objective course of world history leads from feudalism through capitalism to Socialism and Communism, and the 'classless society' is the true aim of human world history, then Socialist praxis prefigures correct and just political praxis. Politics is revolutionary and 'progressive' when it corresponds to the objective tendency of this history; politics is backward and reactionary when it contradicts this history and resists it. The subject of the objective course of world history is the human species. In the present class-society only the exploited irrational proletariat and the oppressed peoples of the Third World represent the interests of all humanity. To organize themselves for their liberation they need the Communist Party which leads them. The cadres of the Party are therefore those who take the necessary steps in the course of world history. The parallel to the old Chinese political religion is obvious: just as the emperor accomplishes the will of heaven on the whole earth under heaven, so the Communist Party accomplishes the will of history in all who live in history. If it fails in its task, then it loses the credentials for its rule and this task must be taken over by others. The ancient Chinese political religion was embedded in the conception of harmony in the scheme of 'nature'. The new political ideology is Marxist-Leninist-Maoist socialism. It is metaphysically embedded in the concept of progress as part of the scheme of 'history'. As a basis for rule, by contrast with the old basis it is atheistic, but in its function of legitimating rule it is religious. It replaces nature mysticism with a mysticism of history. The beyond in heaven above us is replaced by the historical future before us. The fluid equilibrium of Yin and Yang is replaced by the contradictions of history which lead to the class struggle. Mao tried to impress that on the people in the 'cultural revolution'.

The old Tao of nature is re-emerging in the new Tao of history. We can discover further parallels between the old religion and the new political ideology in China. It is presumably more important to see the differences. In theory they lie in the modern suppression of nature from human history and in practice in the exploitation of natural resources and the destruction of nature's powers of regeneration by industry and industrial concentrations. The burden on the environment and the human psyche grows in proportion to the density of population and becomes intolerable after the population of a city reaches around six million. The true future, i.e. the future of the survival of humankind and nature on this earth, therefore does not lie in the continuation of the modern project of 'progress' in the scheme of 'history' but in mediation between this project and the wisdom of the ancient project of 'harmony in the scheme of nature'. The ecological wisdom of the culture of internal and external equilibrium must be translated into historical work on internal and external progress, so that there can be equilibrium between nature and history, harmony and progress. It is therefore not as paradoxical as it might seem that Lao Tsu's book *Tao te Ching* is forgotten in China, having been thought outdated and backward, and at the same time goes through one edition after another in the West, where it is widely circulated and recognized in the ecological movement.

(c) In search of a viable balance between equilibrium and progress

Human history takes place within the cosmic conditions of the earth. Therefore nature cannot be subjected and exploited by human beings without their destroying the basis of their own lives and thus themselves. Nor can it be 'humanized' without collapsing. Nature surrounds and supports human beings and their culture. Human beings can only survive with their culture if they respect the character of nature and its own rights. By nature I mean the ecosystem of earth, which absorbs and processes solar energy through the atmosphere and the biosphere and through the earth's revolutions guarantees the cycles of day and night, summer and winter, rain and sun. The cosmic conditions of the earth are remarkably constant and have made life possible on earth for millions of years. Human cultures, too, have always respected them and adapted to them. The modern project of 'scientific technological civilization' is the first to have suppressed and scorned the natural conditions of life. Today this civilization has reached not only the 'limits of growth' but also the limits of its own conditions of life in the cosmos. If these are irreparably destroyed, then the inhabitants of the earth will die with the ecosystem of earth as we know it – and not just human beings. There can be 'progress in the scheme of history' if the scheme of 'history' is incorporated into a new scheme of 'nature' which picks up the wisdom of the old scheme of 'nature' and transfers it into the framework of the modern scheme of history. This is not an arbitrary, Romantic return to nature, but the necessary ecological progress towards nature. The industrial world cannot survive in its present form, because it profits from destroying nature. The post-industrial world will be the world which is ecologically adapted to nature. A human society capable of survival is conceivable only on the basis of a new equilibrium with nature. This transition from the industrial to the post-industrial age and from historical progress to the new equilibrium with the natural conditions for human civilization is regarded by some scholars as a 'turning point' (F.Capra) and understood in terms of the ancient Chinese concepts of Yin and Yang: after the Yang age, which is male, demanding, aggressive, rational and analytical, will come the Yin age, which has the more female characteristics of conservation, empathy and synthesis. Whereas the Yang action was related to the ego, the new Yin action is in tune with the environment. The transition follows automatically and happens in a gentle way: 'After the Yang has reached its peak it withdraws in favour of the Yin; if the Yin has reached a peak, it withdraws in favour of the Yang', we find in the *I Ching*. The absurd accumulation of the potential for nuclear destruction, the increasing annihilation of animal species and plants, the exhaustion of the life-force of nature and the mass annihilation of human life among the hungry people of the Third World prove with fatal certainty the hopeless end of a human age. The destructive contradictions of 'scientific-technological civilization' in the modern project of history can no longer be coped with by the immanent forces in this project. It is not the further integration of nature into the human history of progress, but conversely only the integration of the human history of progress into the rhythms and cycles of the ecosystem, that can guarantee survival. If we are looking for a

99

balance between human culture and the earth's nature which serves the survival of both, we should abandon any centralism, since such a balance cannot be defined either anthropocentrically or cosmocentrically. Instead of centralistic conceptions the dimensions of a federation are more helpful, because there human interests are also balanced. A federation between culture and nature need not fix relations in a rigid way but can shape the 'interchange of matter' and the mutual interpenetration of the two spheres rhythmically, with changing foci.

The Taoist harmony with nature through the integration of humankind into nature and activity through non-intervention in nature which we find in ancient Chinese culture comes very close to the modern quest for a culture which is capable of survival. 'Not acting against nature encourages the flourishing of things' (*Tao te Ching* 43). The mythical conception of the earth as 'mother of the ten thousand beings' contains that wisdom which arises from insight into the ecological conditions of life on earth: 'Anyone who has found his mother has recognized himself as her son' (52). Human beings are not 'lords and owners of nature' but 'children' of the ecosystem 'earth'. In *wuwei*, activity through not acting, but being there intensively, we have a reflection of the wisdom of the biblical sabbath: 'It gives them life and rears them. It gives them life yet claims no possession; it benefits them yet exacts no gratitude; it is the steward yet exercises no authority. Such is called the mysterious virtue' (10). The gentle shift from 'hard technology' to 'soft technology' is foreshadowed in ch.76: 'A man is supple and weak when living, but hard and stiff when dead… Thus the hard and strong are comrades of death; and the supple and weak are the comrades of life.' 'In the world there is nothing more submissive and weak than water. Yet for attacking that which is hard and strong nothing can surpass it. This is because there is nothing that can take its place' (78).

Modern 'scientific technological civilization' has so far encouraged centralized organization. Industrial areas, industrial conglomerations, concentrations and mass conurbations,

100

the central energy-generating forces, and so on, burden the natural environment and destroy it. The denser the industrial areas, the quicker the forest dies, the more impure the water becomes, and therefore the more poisoned the air is. So there is no meaningful progress in the further centralization of industrial power. If the project of human history is to survive, civilization must be decentralized. Modern techniques of communication make ponderous central administrations superfluous. The new possibilities of using solar energy will replace the central provision of energy. That will also make possible the decentralization of social and political organizations. Districts will become more independent of central government and local communities will become more independent of the regional governments. Life in manageable communities will overcome human isolation and alienation. The Taoist ideal 'A small land, a people small in number... there are weapons there but no reason to take them up...' (80) is not an unrealistic idyll. E.F.Schumacher adopted it in his influential book *Small is Beautiful* and applied it to the healing of wounds in the modern mass conurbations.

4. The scheme of 'history' arises out of the contradictions of the class struggle and in its socialist form is the practical theory of the liberation of humankind by the proletariat's liberation of itself. If this battle is successful in one country and – as in modern China – the class war can be said to have been ended because there are no more classes, then it is appropriate to move that dialectic of struggle over contradictions into the peaceful dialectic of Yin and Yang so as to treat the 'non-antagonistic contradictions' in the new society no longer as conflicts but as mutually supplementary movements in the fluid equilibrium of life. The ancient Chinese way of thinking in dynamic harmonies full of tension is again of inestimable significance for the new paradigm of society brought into a balance with the nature of earth which enables it to survive and to this extent is the paradigm of a post-industrial society.

Notes

I Does Modern Society Have a Future?

1. There are instances in R.North, *Real Cost*, London 1986.

2. Cf. R.Lester Brown et al., *The State of the World. A Worldwatch Institute Report on Progress Toward a Sustainable Society*, New York 1987.

3. Thus also *Economic Justice for All. Catholic Social Doctrine and the US Economy. Pastoral Letter of the Catholic Bishops' Conference of the USA*, National Conference of Catholic Bishops 1986. Unfortunately in this good declaration on economic and social justice there is no perspective on ecological justice. But without that there can be no lasting economic and social justice.

4. See also *Our Common Future. The Brundtland Report of the World Commission on Environment and Development*, London 1987.

II The Nuclear Situation: The Theology and Politics of Peace

1. Martin Luther King Jr, *An Ebony Picture Biography*, Chicago 1968, 43.

2. 'Armageddon and the End Times', TIME, 5 November 1984, 73. See *Armageddon haunts Reagan, Convergence. Report from the Christic Institute, Washington DC, Winter 1985*; R.Jewett, 'Coming to Terms with the Doom Boom', *Methodist Quarterly Review* 1984, 3/4, 9-22.

3. G.M.Martin, *Weltuntergang. Gefahr und Sinn apokalyptischer Visionen*, Stuttgart 1984; L.Reinisch, *Das Spiel mit der Apokalypse. Über die letzten Tage der Menschheit*, Freiburg 1984; U.H.J.Körtner, *Weltangst und Weltende. Eine theologische Interpretation der Apokalyptik*, Göttingen 1988.

4. Cf. the pop apocalyptic of the best-seller by Hal Lindsey, *The Late Great Planet Earth*, New York 1970; he decks out the apocalyptic route to 'Armageddon' with strategic plans by the Russians and the Chinese to invade Jerusalem (144, 148); there these armies will be destroyed by US nuclear bombs, whereupon Christ 'the lion' will appear with his own, who will previously have been 'raptured', in order to set up the millennium on earth.

5. G.Anders, *Die atomare Drohung* (1959), fourth edition, with a preface on 'End Time and End of Times' (1959), Munich 1983; K.Jaspers, *Die Atombombe und die Zukunft der Menschen*, Munich 1958.

6. G.Anders, 'Atomarer Mord – kein Selbstmord' (1959), ibid., 55f.

7. See Chapter I, n.4 above.

8. Cf. J.B.Metz, *Theology of the World*, London 1969; J.B.Metz, J.Moltmann, H.W.Richardson, W.Oelmüller, M.D.Bryant, *Religion and Political Society*, New

York 1974; J.Moltmann, *On Human Dignity. Political Theology and Ethics*, London and New York 1984; D.Sölle, *Politische Theologie*, Stuttgart (1971) 1982.

9. J.Moltmann (ed.), *Friedenstheologie – Befreiungstheologie. Analysen – Berichte – Meditationen*, Munich 1988.

10. G.Anders, op.cit., 20, 22.

11. Ibid., preface to the second edition, ix.

12. Ibid., 217ff.

13. Thus rightly G.M.Martin, *Weltuntergang* (n.3 above), 103.

14. Cf. H.Jonas, 'Der Gottesbegriff nach Auschwitz', in F.Stern and H.Jonas, *Reflexionen in finsterer Zeit*, Tübingen 1984, 61-86. See the Christian answer by E.Jüngel, 'Gottes ursprüngliches Anfangen als schöpferische Selbstbegrenzung Gottes', in *Gottes Zukunft – Zukunft der Welt*, FS J.Moltmann, Munich 1986, 26-75.

15. E.Wiesel, 'Der Mitleidende', in R.Walter (ed.), *Die hundert Namen Gottes. Tore zum letzten Geheimnis*, Freiburg 1985, 70-5.

16. J.Moltmann, *The Crucified God*, London and New York 1974.

17. W.H.Vanstone, *Love's Endeavour, Love's Expense*, London 1977, 120.

18. D.Sölle, *To Work and to Love. A Theology of Creation*, Philadelphia 1984, 209f.

19. R.Rubenstein, *After Auschwitz. Radical Theology and Contemporary Judaism*, New York 1966. See M.Brocke and H.Jochum, *Wolkensäule und Feuerschein, Jüdisches Theologisches Holocaust*, Munich 1982.

20. E.Fackenheim, *God's Presence in History. Jewish Affirmations and Philosophical Reflections*, New York 1970; id., *To Mend the World. Foundations of Future Jewish Thought*, New York 1982. See E.Kogon and J.B.Metz, *Gott nach Auschwitz*, Freiburg 1979.

21. R.Hochhuth, *The Representative*, London 1963, Act 5.

22. M.Horkheimer, *Die Sehnsucht nach dem ganz Anderen*, Hamburg 1970, 61f.

23. W.Benjamin, *Illuminationen. Ausgewählte Schriften*, Frankfurt 1961, 270.

24. B.Moltmann (ed.), *Perspektiven der Friedensforschung*, Schriftenreihe der AG für Friedens- und Konfliktforschung XV, Baden-Baden 1988, is an admirable source of information on peace research today.

25. Thus rightly H.Falcke, 'Theologie des Friedens in einer geteilten Welt', in J.Moltmann (ed.), *Friedenstheologie-Befreiungstheologie* (n.9 above), 45f.

26. Thus Archbishop Cyril of Smolensk at the international peace seminar in Budapest, December 1987.

III   The Ecological Situation: The Theology and Ethics of Creation

1. I am taking these ideas from my book *God in Creation. An Ecological Doctrine of Creation*, London and New York 1985, and developing them further. For the theme see also G.Liedke, *Im Bauch des Fisches. Ökologische Theologie*, Stuttgart ³1983; A.Auer, *Umweltethik. Ein theologischer Beitrag zur ökologischen Diskussion*, Düsseldorf 1984; K.M.Meyer-Abich, *Wege zum Frieden mit der Natur. Praktische Naturphilosophie für die Umweltpolitik*, Munich 1984.

2. See C.Merchant, *The Death of Nature. Women, Ecology and the Scientific Revolution*, San Francisco 1980.

3. I have developed this further in *The Trinity and the Kingdom of God. The Doctrine of God*, London and New York 1981. Cf. also L.Boff, *Trinity and Society*, London 1986, who has taken up my theses on the doctrine of the Trinity and applied them to the church and society.

4. W.Heisenberg, *Der Teil und das Ganze. Gespräche im Umkreis der Atomphysik*, Munich 1969, 324f. He is followed by F.Capra, *The Tao of Physics*, London 1975; id., *The Turning Point*, 1982; id., *Uncommon Wisdom. Conversations with Remarkable People*, New York 1988.

5. Hildegard von Bingen, *Lieder*, Salzburg 1969, 228; see M.Fox, *Illuminations of Hildegard of Bingen*, Santa Fe 1985.

6. Words by Timothy Rees, *Hymns and Psalms*, Methodist Publishing House 1983, no. 36.

7. The initial conceptions of the nature of experimentation in the natural sciences show the use of the interrogatory methods of the torture chambers of the Inquisition to 'wrest its secrets' from nature and 'answer human questions', as Kant still wrote in the preface to the second edition of the *Critique of Pure Reason*.

8. See the influential article by G.von Rad, 'The Theological Problem of the Old Testament Doctrine of Creation' (1936), in *The Problem of the Hexateuch*, Edinburgh 1966 reissued London 1984, 131-43.

9. G.von Rad, *Old Testament Theology* II, Edinburgh 1965 reissued London 1975, 389. He later corrected his view when he discovered the theological significance of the Old Testament wisdom literature: *Wisdom in Israel*, London and Nashville 1972.

10. For more detail see J.Moltmann, *The Way of Jesus Christ. Christology in Messianic Dimensions*, Chapter 6, 'The Cosmic Christ', London and New York 1990 (forthcoming).

11. G.M.Teusch, *Mensch und Tier. Lexikon der Tierschutzethik*, Göttingen 1987.

12. E.Cardenal, *To Live and to Love*, New York 1971.

13. J.Calvin, *Institutes of the Christian Religion* I, 5, 1.

14. Gestalt therapy is now giving rise to a new understanding of the body which can be described as the 'return of the body'. Cf. D.Kamper and C.Wulf, *Die Wiederkehr des Körpers*, Frankfurt 1982; H.Petzold (ed.), *Leiblichkeit. Philosophische, gesellschaftliche und therapeutische Perspektiven*, Paderborn 1985.

15. For Lao Tse, *Tao te Ching*, see the translation by D.C.Lau, Penguin Classics, Harmondsworth 1965 (reprinted twenty-one times).